letters to a young lawyer

The Art of Mentoring from Basic Books

Letters to a Young Lawyer
Alan Dershowitz

Letters to a Young Contrarian
Christopher Hitchens

Letters to a Young Golfer
Bob Duval

Letters to a Young Conservative
Dinesh D'Souza

Letters to a Young Activist
Todd Gitlin

Letters to a Young Therapist
Mary Pipher

Letters to a Young Chef
Daniel Boulud

Letters to a Young Gymnast
Nadia Comaneci

Letters to a Young Catholic
George Weigel

Letters to a Young Actor
Robert Brustein

Also by Alan Dershowitz

Rights from Wrongs: A Secular Theory of the Origins of Rights

America on Trial: Inside the Legal Battles that Transformed our Nation

The Case for Israel

America Declares Independence

Shouting Fire: Civil Liberties in a Turbulent Age

Why Terrorism Works:
Understanding the Threat, Responding to the Challenge

Supreme Injustice: How the High Court Hijacked Election 2000

The Genesis of Justice: 10 Stories of Biblical Injustice That Led to the 10 Commandments and Modern Law

Just Revenge: A Novel

Sexual McCarthyism: Clinton, Starr, and the Emerging Constitutional Crisis

The Vanishing American Jew:
In Search of Jewish Identity for the Next Century

Reasonable Doubts:
The Criminal Justice System and the O.J. Simpson Case

The Abuse Excuse: And Other Cop-Outs, Sob Stories, and Evasions of Responsibility

The Advocate's Devil: A Novel

Contrary to Popular Opinion

Chutzpah

Taking Liberties:
A Decade of Hard Cases, Bad Laws, and Bum Raps

Reversal of Fortune: Inside the Von Bulow Case

The Best Defense

Criminal Law: Theory and Practice
(with Joseph Goldstein and Richard D. Schwartz)

Psychoanalysis, Psychiatry, and Law
(with Jay Katz and Joseph Goldstein)

Alan Dershowitz

letters to a young lawyer

A Member of the Perseus Books Group
New York

This book is lovingly dedicated to
my departed mentors who gave this lawyer
needed advice when he was young:

Judge David Bazelon
Professor Alexander Bickel
Justice William Brennan
Leonard Boudin
Bernard Fischman
Justice Arthur Goldberg
Professor Joseph Goldstein
Professor Telford Taylor
Lewis Weinstein

Hardback edition first published in 2001 by Basic Books,
A Member of the Perseus Books Group
Paperback edition first published in 2005 by Basic Books

Designed by Rick Pracher

A CIP catalog record for this book is available from the Library of Congress.
ISBN 0-465-01631-6 (hc); ISBN 0-465-01633-2 (pbk)

05 06 07 08 / 10 9 8 7 6 5 4 3 2 1

Contents

Acknowledgments

This book could not have been written without input from the generations of students who have sought my advice and then told me, years later, whether it was useful.

My appreciation to Maura Kelly for typing the manuscript, to Peggy Burlet for organizing the effort, to my agent Helen Reiss for persuading me to undertake it, to John Donatich for suggesting the idea, to those who allowed me to borrow from previously published works, to the nice people at Basic Books who facilitated the copyediting and other important aspects of publication.

Finally, a word of love and appreciation to my family for reviewing the manuscript and for all the free advice they give me all the time.

Introduction

Giving advice is among the most hazardous of undertakings. I know because I have received much bad advice and because I have almost certainly given some. During the thirty-seven years I have been teaching law at Harvard, I have probably been asked for advice thousands of times.

Most advice turns out to be a series of instructions about how to become the person who is giving the advice. People seem to have a powerful need to re-create themselves (perhaps that's why we worry so much about cloning). I recall vividly being told by one of my mentors, a distinguished professor, the order in which I should publish several writings I was then contemplating. It soon became clear that he was merely recounting his own publishing biography. He wanted me to become him, just as several of my other mentors wanted me to be them. Supreme Court Justice Arthur Goldberg, for whom I clerked, was always giving me career advice directed toward me becoming a judge — a position to which I did not aspire. Professor Joseph Goldstein, who was my mentor at law school, pressed me to limit myself to academic and theoretical work — but I loved having one foot in the hurly-burly world of practical law and politics.

I believe strongly that imitation is not the highest form of flattery, because truly unique individuals can never be imitated. But you can learn from them, so long as you realize that you are a different person, with your own dreams, backgrounds and priorities. Understand the differences and extrapolate from their experiences and aspirations to your own unique life.

Be careful, however, about accepting anyone's advice — including my own — on the basis of "years of experience." Before you put too much stock in experience, make sure the person offering the advice has learned from his or her own experiences. Most people don't. They simply repeat their mistakes, over and over again. Their "years of experience" are little more than years of making the same mistakes over and over again without realizing that they are mistakes.

It's particularly difficult to know as a lawyer whether you've made mistakes, since there is little correlation between a job well done and a successful outcome. There are simply too many variables at play.

I recall as a young lawyer reading an appellate brief written by an "experienced" lawyer. It contained a section that was anachronistic, citing lines of cases that had been either overruled or disregarded. Moreover, it was poorly argued and even more poorly written. Since he was representing my client's co-defendant, I pressed him about why he had included that section. He told me that he always included that section in every appeal that raised Fourth Amendment issues. "It's based on experience," he assured me. "I've been citing that section for twenty years." I asked him if he had ever won a case based on that section. He paused, thought for a moment, and said "No, not yet." Recently I read another brief by this now elderly lawyer. It contained the same section. He had not learned a thing from his years of mistakes. That kind of experience you can do without.

Also, beware of "wholesale," "off-the-rack" or "one-size-fits-all" advice. The best advice is always retail, custom-made and particular to the person seeking it. Yet there are some general principles that may prove useful so long as they are supplemented by retail advice specific to you.

You may note that although this book is entitled *Letters to a Young Lawyer*, the advice that follows is not conveyed in actual "letters." That is a sign of the times. The written letter used to be a great art form. Rilke's wonderful *Letters to a Young Poet*, which inspire this book, were themselves an extension of his poetry. His soul is visible, even in his hastily written epistolary words. As a product of the postwar technological revolution, I am not a letter writer. Oh sure, I've dictated my share of letters to the editor, demand letters ("Screw you. Tough letter to follow.") and other professional correspondence. But I rarely write personal letters. Even in the current age of the computer, I am not an e-mail addict. Instead, I talk. Almost all of my advice has been oral. Fortunately, I write like I talk. I've never believed that there is a separate language called legalese — at least not a language designed for comprehension. I teach my students that a good brief writer is simply a good writer. I urge those students who speak well but write poorly to listen to their voice. Indeed, I urge them to tape-record their voice and then try to imitate in their writing what they have spoken so eloquently.

And so, what follows is a written rendition of the oral advice I have given over the past nearly forty years. They are oral letters. In writing them, I have in mind the diversity of students, friends, children of friends, friends of children, colleagues and strangers who have asked me for advice over the past several generations. Sometimes I have a particular person in mind when I write. Mostly I envisage composites — men and women, younger and older, successful and unsuccessful, happy and unhappy. Of course, most people who seek advice are not perfectly happy, because people who are rarely need advice from those of us who are not. On the other hand, most of those who have sought advice from me have been more successful than the average lawyer. They have choices to make. Occasionally, I run across a student whose choices are quite limited. The advice they seek often takes the form of the question "Should I give up and get out of the law?" This is the exception. The rule tends to be a request for advice about a considerable number of available options, all of which are good. In contrast to my legal practice of defending mostly guilty criminals, where the options are generally "worse," "worser" and "worsest," the options for my talented and wonderful students are generally "good," "better" and "best."

I realize, too, that some students—particularly my own students — who purport to be seeking *advice* from me are actually soliciting my *help*. They understand, quite shrewdly, that seeking advice is a high form of flattery. They are willing to listen to my opinion, even though they have really made up their own minds and are seeking my assistance in achieving their predetermined goals. They understand that an advice-giver often becomes invested in helping the advisee act on the advice received. For example, students will often ask me my opinion of a particular judge or lawyer to whom they are applying. When I tell them that they would be well advised to work for that person, the next question often is "Can you write me a recommendation?" I think I can recognize the difference between those seeking advice and those seeking assistance. But flattery often blinds, and I suspect that I have sometimes been blinded myself.

Inevitably, all advice is, at least in part, autobiographical. In this book, I try to be conscious of avoiding the mistake of telling you how to become me (not that you would want to!). Many people, over the years, have explicitly asked me how they could design careers like mine. I realize, of course, that my career is unique, and not easily subject to replication. Nor would many people want to have careers of such controversy and polarity. In introducing me to speak last year, someone described me as having "the most fascinating legal practice in the world." I have no idea whether this is true, but I can attest to the incredible diversity of what I do on a daily basis. My typical day can well include teaching a class in criminal law, having lunch with a group of students, taking a call from a death-row inmate, receiving an e-mail from a political dissident halfway around the world, considering a request to testify in front of a Senate committee, writing an op-ed piece for the *New York Times*, appearing on a nationally telecast show, getting a death threat from an irate viewer, giving discreet advice to a corporate executive or politician, consulting with the attorney general of a foreign country, becoming the target of an attack by Rush Limbaugh, Bill O'Reilly or some other right-wing talk-show host, being lectured by my mother and receiving an obscene phone call in the middle of the night complaining about one of my clients.

My clients have included "a Dickensian lineup of suspects" (according to *Fortune Magazine)*, both rich and poor, famous and infamous, loved and hated. I am fortunate in being able to pick and choose from among the nearly five thousand requests for representation I receive each year, and I can afford to select them without regard to whether they can pay a fee. I select only a small number of cases, about half of which are pro bono. They all have one factor in common: I am pissed off by an injustice being perpetrated against the person, whether he or she may be innocent or guilty.

In choosing my clients, I have learned never to confuse celebrities with fascinating people, or high-profile cases with important ones. I turn down many celebrities and high-profile cases in favor of obscure people with no money but an important or compelling issue.

Mine is by no means a typical lawyer's career or a typical law professor's life. Yet because I have partaken in so many different aspects of the life of the contemporary lawyer, I willingly share the insights gained through these adventures in the hope that some may benefit from my mistakes.

My goal in writing this book is to encourage others to learn from my successes and failures, from my correct decisions and my erroneous ones.

Among the questions that I am most often asked are "How did you get to where you are?" and "How did you design the interesting career you have?" The honest answer is "By complete accident." I had no grand plan or careful design, and I had little guidance from others. I started out hoping to become a storefront lawyer in Brooklyn. (My mother even had the store picked out.) Then, when I did well in law school, I decided to become a law professor. Then I decided to take on a few clients in order to broaden my professional background and enhance my teaching skills. Then I decided to write popular columns and articles. Then I decided to write books, which inevitably leads to giving public lectures. Finally I decided that I liked the mix. My lifestyle is certainly not for everyone. I work too hard, offend too many people, generate too much controversy and am too much of a provocateur. In a word, I have too much chutzpah. But I have experienced enough of the diversity of life and law practice so that perhaps my experiences can help others in making choices of their own.

In this book, I offer a mix of practical advice about careers, philosophical ruminations about justice, psychological insights into winning and losing — and even some speculations on whether it is possible to be both an effective professional and a good person (a "mensch," as my mother would put it).

What is most missing from this book is the interactive nature of the conversations I actually have with those to whom I am imparting advice. So let's do the best we can. E-mail me your own reactions to my advice and I will try to respond. In that way we can turn this monologue into a dialogue. My e-mail address is alder@law.harvard.edu. For those, like me, who are not addicted to e-mail, my mailing address is Harvard Law School, 1575 Massachusetts Avenue, Cambridge, MA 02138.

With all these caveats in mind, I plunge feet-forward into the advice-giving business, hoping, perhaps, that I can avoid some of the pitfalls I have experienced, but knowing full well that I will trip over others.

Part ONE

Life and Career

1
Pick Your Heroes Carefully

Lawyers tend to be hero worshippers. Perhaps because we often work on an ethically ambiguous terrain, we need to create larger-than-life role models to look up to. We airbrush the warts of our heroes and turn them into saints who could do no wrong. Eventually, we learn the truth and we become disappointed, if not disillusioned. I know, since I have been through the process on several occasions.

My own legal heroes included Clarence Darrow, Oliver Wendell Holmes, Louis Brandeis, Felix Frankfurter, Hugo Black, William O. Douglas, Thurgood Marshall and William Brennan — as well as the two judges for whom I clerked, David Bazelon and Arthur Goldberg. They also included several of my law professors at Yale and older colleagues at Harvard. I wanted to be like these giants of the law. I grew up in a community and family with few judges or lawyers. I vividly remember asking my immigrant grandmother to introduce me to her friend Judge Berenkoff. She asked me why I wanted to meet Judge Berenkoff. I told her because he is a judge. Grandma laughed and told me that Berenkoff was a butcher. "Then why do you always refer to him as judge?" I asked. "Because that's his name," Grandma said. "Judge – G-E-O-R-G-E," she said, spelling out his first name with her thick Yiddish accent. "Judge" Berenkoff was about as close as I would get to a real judge in my old Brooklyn neighborhood. So, I searched for role models and found them among these judges, practicing lawyers and law professors — some living and some dead.

I read everything I could about my dead heroes. When I was a student, legal biography was generally hagiography. I grew up in an age when most public figures were written about with praise. In my day, Clarence Darrow was beatified in *Attorney for the Damned.* Oliver Wendell Holmes was glorified in *Yankee from Olympus.* Thomas More was the hero of the play and film *A Man for All Seasons.*

I'll never forget the day I saw the great actor Paul Muni portray the great lawyer Clarence Darrow on Broadway in the play *Inherit the Wind.* As I watched "Darrow" (he was called "Drummond") cross-examine "William Jennings Bryant" (he was called "Brady"), I knew precisely what kind of a lawyer I wanted to, and had to, become. I'll also never forget the day many years later when I first learned that Darrow had almost certainly bribed witnesses and jurors in order to secure acquittals or hung juries in criminal cases. I was devastated. My hero not only had clay feet, his entire structure crumbled before me. I had been asked to write a review of a new book on Darrow by Geoffrey Cowan. The author, who was generally sympathetic to his subject, made an overwhelming case that in the interest of leveling the playing field against the large corporations that payed for the conviction of his radical, labor union clients, Darrow had to pay the bribes. I was not persuaded. Whatever Darrow's motives, the convincing evidence that he bribed jurors forever disqualifies Darrow from being a role model for lawyers. There is simply no justification for corrupting the legal system, even if it is done to level the playing field.

In his book, Cowan had written that law schools do not teach about such devices as bribery. In my review, I agreed:

> *The reason we do not teach such "devices" in law school is that they are not lawyers' tools. They may indeed be the tools of revolutionaries and others who work outside the system, and they may perhaps even be justified by a revolutionary means-end calculus. But a lawyer, who does lawyers' work, cannot employ such devices, regardless of the provocation. The lawyer may rail against the corruption of his opponents; the lawyer may expose or condemn — or perhaps even be*

> *right to resign from the practice of law to become a revolutionary, if the cause is just and the provocation sufficient. But the lawyer may not become part of the corruption in order to fight for justice as a lawyer. If Darrow crossed that line, as Cowan convincingly argues he did, then he does not deserve the mantle of honor he has proudly borne over most of this century. Those of us who have long regarded Darrow as a hero will be disappointed to learn of his clay feet, but . . . the harsh claims of history must outweigh any inclination toward hagiography, even when the subject is one of the very few lawyers who have had plausible claims to legal sainthood.*

These academic words, however, concealed a personal disappointment — even grief — that I did not feel comfortable revealing. Unlike the police chief in *Casablanca*, who expressed mock shock at learning there was gambling at Rick's Place, my shock was real and deep. It continued for weeks. I was consumed by how Darrow had tricked me into believing he was the kind of lawyer I wanted to be. Though Darrow was long dead, my anger toward him was very personal — the kind you might feel toward a close friend or lover who has betrayed you. I've never gotten over it.

It wasn't as personal when I learned that most of my other heroes had clay feet — or at least one clay foot. The process of disillusionment was more gradual. I was let down more slowly when I discovered what horrible values Oliver Wendell Holmes had privately espoused in his letters to friends. He favored sterilization — perhaps even murder — of "incompetents." Holmes wrote approvingly of killing "anyone below standard" and "putting to death infants that didn't pass the examination."[1] In upholding the constitutionality of mandatory sterilization laws, he approved the sterilization of a woman who was mistakenly classified as an "imbecile." Thousands of people, many of whom were misdiagnosed, were sterilized pursuant to the Holmes precedent. Even the Nazis cited this precedent in support of their program of racial eugenics.

My anger at Felix Frankfurter, whose chair I currently occupy at Harvard, was pretty intense when I read about his refusal to help the Jews of Europe during the Holocaust, but I had already met Justice Frankfurter by that time, and I didn't like him — I found him to be petty and sycophantic — so the disappointment was muted. Not so with Justice Black, who I knew had been a member of the Ku Klux Klan before his elevation to the High Court, but who I thought had gotten over his early racism. Then he spoke to a group of law clerks during the year I was clerking on the Supreme Court, and it became evident that he still had some lingering racial bias. He also struck me as an extremely rigid man, not open to new ideas. Justice Douglas, who was open to ideas, was nasty to the law clerks, the secretaries and the other court personnel. He also got into a fight with Judge David Bazelon, for whom I had clerked, which revealed something about him that surprised me. Bazelon had been asked to speak at a private club to which Douglas belonged. The club excluded Jews and blacks. Bazelon, who was Jewish, declined the invitation, saying that he would not speak at a club that he, and others, would not be eligible to join. Douglas called him on the phone and started to berate him for his "narrow-mindedness." Bazelon signaled me to pick up the other receiver and listen. I couldn't believe what I was hearing. Here was this paragon of racial and religious equality, trying to convince my boss to compromise his principles and speak to a segregated club. Bazelon stuck to his guns, and Douglas slammed down the phone in anger.

My other heroes — Louis Brandeis, Thurgood Marshall and William Brennan — had lesser faults, but still, when I learned about them I was disappointed. Brandeis had engaged in some ethically questionable behavior as a lawyer, because he sometimes considered himself "counsel to the situation," rather than advocate for a particular client. Marshall was often poorly prepared when he argued cases, even important ones in the Supreme Court. Brennan refused to hire women law clerks for many years, and fired a law clerk — at the insistence of Chief Justice Earl Warren — when the clerk's left-wing activities became the subject of critical media reports. I still admire these three justices enormously, even with the knowledge that they weren't perfect.

The same is true of the two judges for whom I worked. When you interact with someone on a daily basis, their virtues and their vices become magnified. "No one is a hero to his butler," says an old English saw, and no judge can ever be a flawless saint to his law clerks. But Judge David Bazelon and Justice Arthur Goldberg both served as imperfect role models for me in many important ways, as have some of my professors and older colleagues.

So please, no heroes and no worship. Look up to people who have admirable traits, but understand that all have human foibles, some more than others. Expect to be disappointed, especially if you ever get to know personally those you look up to. Learn to live with the disappointments and still emulate those characteristics of your role models that warrant emulation. But even singular characteristics will rarely be without flaws.

Law is an imperfect profession in which success can rarely be achieved without some sacrifice of principle.[2] Thus all practicing lawyers — and most others in the profession — will necessarily be imperfect, especially in the eyes of young idealists. There is no perfect justice, just as there are no absolutes in ethics. But there is perfect injustice, and we know it when we see it.

I can only imagine how so many law students, who were taught to revere the justices of our Supreme Court, must have reacted when they came to believe that five of the justices violated their oaths of office by stopping the Florida hand count in the 2000 presidential election. The judicial oath requires each justice to swear "to administer justice without regard to persons. . . ."

Despite this oath, the five justices — in complete disregard of their prior decisions and writings — stopped the count in order to ensure the election of a particular person — George W. Bush. They never would have stopped the count under the identical legal circumstances if the result would have been to ensure the election of Al Gore. If you do not believe that, consider the following law school hypo: Imagine if, six months before the election case, 1,000 of the most prominent constitutional law professors, Supreme Court litigators and journalists who cover the High Court had been given an approximation of the majority opinion in the Florida case. Only here's the twist. The names of the litigants and their party affiliations were not provided.

Is there anyone who believes the experts would have predicted how the five justices actually wound up voting? To the contrary, most surely would have predicted that, on the basis of their prior decisions, Chief Justice William Rehnquist and Justices Antonin Scalia, Clarence Thomas and Sandra Day O'Connor would have been the least likely to join such a decision. After all, these judges have repeatedly ruled that the same equal protection clause is *not* violated when the state executes convicted murderers on the basis of far less precise standards. Had Vice President Al Gore been ahead by a few hundred votes and Governor George W. Bush been seeking a recount, I have no doubt these justices would have mocked any equal protection claim made by Gore.

If I am right, then what else could this be but administering justice *with* regard to persons? To render judgment based on personal or partisan politics — on the party affiliations of the litigants — is to violate the first rule of judging. Never decide a case on the basis of favoritism.

I have written about this decision in considerable detail elsewhere.[3] Here my point is somewhat different. It is about the disillusionment that comes with learning that some justices actually cheat. You probably already suspected that some lower court judges play favorites with lawyers and litigants who supported their election or appointment. But Supreme Court justices? That came as a surprise even to a lifelong cynic like me. What does this revelation do to your commitment to the rule of law? Does it give *you* license to cheat?

My hope is that it redoubles your commitment to the rule of law and to total honesty in its practice. It should also make you more suspicious of all legal and judicial institutions. Trust no one in power, including — especially — judges. Don't take judicial opinions at face value. Go back and read the transcript. Cite-check the cases. You will be amazed at how often you will find judges "finessing" the facts and the law. Too often, legal observers take as a given judges' intellectual honesty. It's up to you to do a better job. If you smell a rat, blow the whistle to the Judicial Conference, the American Bar Association, Congress. At the same time, protect yourself from accusations of unprofessional conduct by being absolutely sure of your criticism (never forget that judges and lawyers protect one another).

In the meantime, get real. Understand that judges are human beings and that in American most of them have gotten where they are by playing the partisan political game, and playing it well. The best check on the judiciary is a suspicious consumer.

It must start in law school. It must start with you.

Having said all of this, I must admit that I still have one perfect hero. He was a lawyer, but his heroism took place primarily outside of his professional role. I even met him and got to know him a bit, and yet his status as hero has not diminished one iota. His name is not widely known, and his particular heroism can never be replicated — at least I hope not. His name is Jan Karski, and he died in July 2000 at the age of eighty-six. When he was a twenty-eight-year-old lawyer-diplomat in Poland, this young Catholic school graduate went undercover into Jewish ghettos and death camps in order to report on the horrible, indeed lethal, conditions. He was captured by the Gestapo and tortured. After escaping, he went back to the death camps, risking his life repeatedly. He pulled out his own teeth in order to change his appearance and avoid detection. He might have saved hundreds of thousands of lives by disclosing the reality of what was happening in Nazi-occupied Poland. But when he was smuggled out of Poland with his detailed information, he was taken to see the most important Jew in

Washington — a Jew who was close to President Franklin Roosevelt — Justice Felix Frankfurter. With a great lawyer's memory for detail, Karski reported on his visits to the ghettos and the death camps, giving specifics. Frankfurter refused to relate the information to Roosevelt, saying he could not believe what Karski was reporting. The reality is that Frankfurter did not want to risk his friendship and influence with Roosevelt by putting his own credibility behind a report that he thought Roosevelt might not believe. That is the difference between a true hero and a deeply flawed man of influence. Understand that difference and live by it.

2
Live the Passion of Your Times

Passion should not be reserved for the bedroom. It must extend to your life's work. You will spend far more time and energy working than making love — or playing sports, eating or listening to opera. Yet the common advice for lawyers is to be dispassionate, removed, objective, detached — in a word, professional. There is no inconsistency between passion and professionalism, so long as each is employed appropriately.

Passion is the motivator. Professionalism is the means by which the task is carried out. Even if the means requires objectivity and detachment, passion can stimulate the best use of these tools.

Sometimes your passion should be out there for all to see. An effective lawyer can use passion — selectively and with modulation — as a tool of advocacy. But don't overuse it, or it will diminish its impact, like the boy crying "wolf."

Beyond its value in the legal profession, passion is important as a life force. I have seen lawyers become so detached, removed and dispassionate in their work that they can no longer do anything with passion. Professional detachment takes over their lives.

Gilbert and Sullivan's *Mikado* condemned those who praised every century but their own. The poet Edward Arlington Robinson created a character, Miniver Cheevy, who "loved the days of old" and "sighed for what was not." Many seek escape from the present in science fiction, history and fantasy. Justice Holmes got it right when he urged his fellow lawyers to live the passion of their times. There's an old Chinese curse: "May you live in interesting times." For me, that has always been a blessing. With the exceptions of cataclysmic eras, such as the Holocaust, every individual is capable of making his or her time interesting or routine. It's largely a matter of attitude.

Recently, I received a very gratifying letter from a former student that spoke directly to this issue. With his permission, let me quote from it:

Dear Professor Dershowitz:

About six years, I had the good fortune of having you as my small-section Criminal Law professor. As you can probably guess from the letterhead, after my Harvard education, I did not go on to practice criminal law. I did, though, take some advice that you repeatedly gave us during that class: I went on to carve out a niche for myself practicing what I love (which, for me, ended up being labor and employment law).

When you first encourage us to carve out our own career paths, I was not sure how applicable your advice would be for me. I knew I would likely end up in a large firm: I also knew that most of my initial assignments would be dictated for me by the firm's partners. But when I finally landed at Porter Wright, I decided I would try to carve out my own practice niche, because Porter Wright was receptive to my initiative I came to work every day much as you used to come to class: thrilled to be a lawyer.

A few months ago, a colleague of mine asked me to name my favorite Harvard Law School professors. I had many favorites, and my friend was not surprised by most of my choices. When I identified you, though, my friend (who did not have you as a professor) raised his eyebrows. He knows me to be politically conservative, and I think he was a bit taken aback that I would identify someone having political convictions so different from my own. But my reasons for identifying you have nothing to do with your political views. As I explained to my friend, you gave me the best advice I received from any professor at Harvard Law School. And, more than most professors, you demonstrated every day that you loved being a lawyer.

(This nice letter is more than matched by the daily hate mail my office receives from an assortment of kooks, bigots and outraged citizens, many of which are unprintable. A recent printable letter from an old Harvard alum — who was not one of my students — states that I remind people of "a nasty and vicious Woody Allen" and that I "exploit" my students by not paying them when they work for me. I pay them out of my own pocket.)

A law student once asked Judge Benjamin Cardozo, then on the New York Court of Appeals, why he got all the interesting cases. He replied that the cases were not particularly interesting until he started to think about them. I observed that phenomenon with Judge Bazelon, who managed to turn the most mundane criminal cases into vehicles for raising the most profound legal and moral issues of criminal responsibility, the role of defense counsel and the relationship between poverty and crime. His passion was reflected in his opinions and his life's work. It was also contagious, and many young lawyers who worked for him caught it. I know I did.

3
Have a Good Enemies' List

Your mother told you it's important to have the right friends. But it's equally important to have the right enemies. Pick your enemies as carefully as your friends. A really good enemies' list is often a sure sign of a courageous and moral person. The world is full of evil people and it is important to stand up to evil. As Edmund Burke said, "All that is necessary for evil to succeed is for good people to remain silent." Martin Niemoeller, an opponent of Nazi racial ideology in the Lutheran church and one of the founders of the oppositional Confessional Church, personally experienced this phenomenon:

> *First they came for the Communists, but I was not a Communist so I did not speak out. Then they came for the Socialists and the Trade Unionists, but I was neither, so I did not speak out. Then they came for the Jews, but I was not a Jew so I did not speak out. And*

when they came for me, there was no one left to speak out for me.

In the world in which we live today, a lawyer without any enemies is likely to be a coward and a sycophant. A lawyer with the right enemies is often an advocate who has taken on powerful interests and stood up for the poor, the disenfranchised and the despised.

Don't try to become a "Sara Lee" lawyer. Remember the slogan: "Nobody doesn't like Sara Lee." Of course not. It's a cake! You're a lawyer in an adversarial system. If everybody likes you, you're doing something wrong. You're not being tough enough. You're not taking on controversial cases. You're putting your friendship with other lawyers above the interests of your clients. You're sucking up.

I'm not proposing that you be gratuitously offensive. I know I sometimes am. As my mother says, "You catch more flies with honey than with vinegar." Though we're not in the fly-catching business, it is often better to use friendship than enmity to serve the interests of your clients. But enmity is sometimes inevitable in an adversarial world. So be selective in your choice of enemies. Know the difference between who you want to like you and who you want to hate you. A person should be judged, at least in part, by the enemies he or she keeps.

4 Don't Do What You're Best At

Some of the least happy people I know are those who figure out what they are best at and then tailor the job to their particular expertise. The problem is that what you're best at is not necessarily what gives you the most gratification or what is most important. Our educational system steers students toward courses and areas in which they excel. Grades are, after all, quite important to getting into college and law school. And it's OK to take courses in which you will excel. But courses last only a few months. Life is forever. So pick a career, or an area within your career, that balances excellence and gratification. It should challenge you every day and have you waking up eager to confront the day's challenges. Obviously, you don't want to pick something you're not very good at, no matter how much you might enjoy it (for me, that would be basketball). Pick an area that you're quite good at but that gives you so much joy that you can't wait to get up in the morning and go to work.

Early in my career, when I was less controversial, I was offered law school deanships and university presidencies. I knew enough about myself to turn them down. In one instance I wrote a "Groucho Marx" reply, saying that I would not want to join a club — or in this case, a school — that would have me as its dean. A dean or president must be able to bring people together. I drive them apart. I am a provocateur, not a pacifier. I would enjoy the prestige of being a dean, a president or perhaps a judge, but I would hate the day-to-day aspects of the job.

I know too many people who have taken prestigious jobs — deanships, chairmanships, judgeships, professorships, partnerships — simply because they were flattered to be offered them. Understand the difference between being offered a job and accepting it. It *is* flattering, even career-enhancing, to *be offered* a prestigious job, but it is a terrible mistake to *accept* the job unless it is right for you — at the stage of life you are at when it is offered.

Having said that, another word of caution: Don't love your work too much, especially if you're a lawyer. When I was a young lawyer, my elders would talk about the law being a jealous mistress or loving the law. Don't love the law. It will inevitably disappoint you. Understand that the law is a tool, a mechanism, a construct. It is a false idol like so many others in life. In one respect, there really is no such thing as "The Law." What we call the law is a process, a group of people, some ideas, precedents, books. Don't respect the law, unless it merits your respect. The law in Nazi Germany or in apartheid

South Africa or in the Jim Crow South did not deserve respect. The Supreme Court's decision in *Bush v. Gore* should be followed — that's what it means to live under the rule of law. But it should not be respected, any more than the robed cheaters who wrote it should be respected. American law today sometimes deserves respect, other times it deserves condemnation. It must always be obeyed, but it need not be admired. Honesty is more important than respect.

If you don't love the law, what should you love (aside from loved *ones*)? Love liberty. Love justice. Love the good that law can produce. Aspirations don't disappoint, so long as you realize that the struggle for liberty, justice and anything else worth pursuing never stays won.

5
Don't Have Deathbed Regrets

We've all heard the cliché that "nobody on their death bed ever regretted not having spent more time at the office." Sure! *If* you achieved a high degree of professional and financial success during your lifetime. But the reality is that there are many people who *should* regret not having spent more time at work. These are the people who failed to achieve their potential because of laziness or misplaced priorities. We rarely hear *their* deathbed regrets: "Damn, I should have spent more time working and less time with my ungrateful kids and the wife who left me for a more successful guy."

The reality is that the frustration growing out of failure to meet your professional goals may well hurt your family and personal life. At least for some, there is a direct relationship between professional success and family happiness. This is not to deny that many successful people spend far too much time making more and more money and far too little time enjoying it with their family.

Striking an appropriate balance between professional and family life is one of the most difficult challenges faced by professionals. Nor is there any one correct balance for everyone. Each individual must decide on the priorities appropriate for him or her.

"To everything there is a season," as Ecclesiastes wrote, and priorities may differ over time. When aspiring for partnership, it may be wise to spend more time in the office — perhaps even to postpone becoming a parent, or to shift primary child-rearing responsibilities to the spouse who is not in the rat race for partnership. For some couples, gender may be a factor, while for others the choice of priorities may be gender-neutral.

I have observed a generation-skipping phenomenon among some of my friends and students. First-generation lawyers — especially those whose parents were working-class immigrants with little formal education — tended to choose hard work and professional success over hands-on involvement in child rearing. The children of such highly motivated and successful professionals often tend to choose the opposite priorities, because they were both the victims and the beneficiaries of their parents' — most often their fathers' — priorities: They were victims of less hands-on parental involvement in their own upbringing, and they were beneficiaries of the financial security achieved by their parents' hard work. They want to avoid victimizing their own children in the way they believe their own parents — in their drive for success — victimized them. They, themselves, need and value financial success less, because their parents have provided them with the kind of safety net whose absence made their parents work so hard.

These generational dynamics obviously differ among families, but every family has its own action-reaction phenomenon. The point is that the decision about priorities will be influenced by many factors, some conscious and some unconscious. But it should *be* a *decision!* All too often priorities are not explicitly chosen, they just seem to happen. And only years later —hopefully well before the clichéd deathbed regret scene — do we come to realize the choices made, the priorities chosen, the road taken. By then it is often too late to return to the illusory fork in the road and to explore the one not taken.

Yet, to some extent we all obsess about that mysterious road. That is why Frost's poem continues to have such a hold over our imagination. The road not taken almost always seems more inviting — perhaps because its bumps are not as palpable as those on the road we took. For some the obsession becomes debilitating — that's all they think about. I have a close family member who stays awake at night wondering how different her life would have been if only. . . . She realizes it is a waste of emotional energy, but she can't help it. The reality, of course, is that there are few well-marked forks on the actual road of life. They only appear as forks after it is too late to return to them. The important forks are those that remain before us. And we must learn to recognize them based on our experience in missing the earlier ones.

One clue is to understand the difference between a genuine fork in the road and a temporary shift in priorities. Every decision has consequences and few are entirely reversible, but there is a considerable difference between those kinds of decisions that lead to a point of no return and those that simply slow down progress toward one goal in the interest of another. An example of the former would be leaving a large law firm while well along the partnership track in order to go to Hollywood and write scripts. Even David Kelley — the most successful law scriptwriter of the age —could not now return to the partnership track of most major institutional law firms. An example of the latter would be to take a leave from a big firm to accept a position in government — or perhaps to help raise a child.

The Greek philosophers extolled the life of balance. Two and a half millennia later, we still have not devised the perfect formula for achieving it. That is so because the formula is different for each individual, and because none of us has been given the gift of perfect insight into our own life and foresight as to the priorities that will maximize its fulfillment. Life is an adventure, with no preordained course. We will all make mistakes, do things and fail to do things we regret. The best we can hope for is to learn from our experiences and not to obsess over our bad choices. There are no do-overs in life, but you do generally get more than one strike. So think about your likely deathbed regrets well before that fateful day, and do something to avoid them.

6
Don't Follow "Off-the-Rack" Advice

Start your own firm. Work your way up to partner in a big firm. Join a small boutique. Be a government lawyer. Do public interest work. Run for Congress. Write Hollywood screenplays. Go into business. Write for a newspaper. Become an investment banker.

I'm sure you've been given most, if not all, of the above advice. I know professors and other lawyers who give the same "off-the-rack" standard advice to everyone who asks — and even some who don't. But as I've said, advice, if it's to be useful, has to be tailor-fitted to each individual person. There are some young lawyers who are born to be big-firm partners. They have the temperaments and skills necessary to reach the top of the bureaucratic ladder. Others are solo practitioners by nature. They thrive on the independence of working alone, without supervision or hierarchy. Still others belong in government jobs. They need to wear the white hats and the flag on their lapels. Some must oppose the government, the corporation and all other authority figures. The great thing about law is that it is a job that fits almost every need. And if there isn't an existing job, you can create it. That's certainly what I've tried to do in my own life.

But don't accept advice that reflects the personalities and priorities of the advice givers, unless you want to be like them. Figure out which kind of situation best suits you as a unique individual with very particular needs and tastes. There is no career path that suits everyone. There is no one right way, though there certainly are some wrong ways. The worst way is to try to fit yourself into someone else's job description. Live in your own skin, not someone else's.

It's OK to do someone else's job for a limited period of time as a means toward another end. Sure, go to work for a big firm in order to learn how they do things even if you know you're not suited to that kind of life. But be sure to have an exit strategy and timetable, lest you be trapped by inertia, and by becoming dependent on the seductively huge salaries and staff support that are more typical of big firms than of most other forms of legal practice.

Another good thing about a legal career is that you can try different things, either one at a time or sometimes even at the same time. Some of my former students have tried the big firm, government, the corporation, the small firm and politics — all within the sphere of a decade. Others have written novels or screenplays while working at a firm. You don't want to develop a reputation as a dilettante, but the line between a "dilettante" and a "renaissance person" may be in the eye of the beholder.

7
Don't Limit Your Options by Making a Lot of Money

There is a disturbing phenomenon that I have observed over the years among friends and former students. All their lives they aspire toward a particular dream job, say a judgeship or a professorship or a job as a top prosecutor. In the meantime, they go to work in a law firm, achieving partnership and a high salary.

Now, finally, they are offered their dream job. But they feel that they now have to decline it because they "can't afford" the salary cut. Ten years earlier, when they were making much less money, they could have afforded their dream job and they would have taken it immediately if it had been offered. Had they accepted the job *then*, they would now have *less* money in the bank. Now they have *more* money in the bank, but they can't afford to fulfill their life's dream, because they have become accustomed to a high standard of living.

If wealth is measured, at least in part, by one's ability to afford certain desirable objects, then the irony is that my friends who turned down judgeships or other dream jobs were richer when they had less money and poorer when they had more.

It is crazy to let wealth stand in the way of your dreams. Of course, economists talk about "opportunity costs" and in that sense, it "costs" more to accept a $150,000-a-year judgeship when you're earning $500,000 than it was when you were earning $175,000. But even back then — when you would have taken the judgeship — you would have been foregoing the opportunity to earn the $500,000 you are now making. So then from a purely economic perspective you are better off today accepting the judgeship *after* having earned a lot more money in the intervening years. The difference is largely psychological or lifestyle. Now that you have gotten used to the $500,000-a-year lifestyle, it's a lot harder to go back to $150,000 (plus the income from what you've saved). Your dream job may look different now, because you're older and more mature. That's OK. But if it looks different only because of the money, there's something wrong. And are you sure that you can really tell the difference?

Unless you prefer your incrementally higher lifestyle over your dream job, don't let your wealth make you unable to afford what you could have afforded when you were poorer. That's just nuts!

This is part of the much larger question of why lawyers — at least elite big-firm lawyers — make so much money. I'm not begrudging them their phenomenally high incomes — except in comparison with other professionals (like schoolteachers, nurses, psychologists, social workers) who do so much good and are paid so little. We live in a market-driven economy where supply and demand determine compensation. My focus here is not on the fairness of the system, but rather on its impact on career choices. Money distorts priorities. Don't get me wrong. Money matters, and there's nothing wrong with wanting to live a comfortable, even financially independent life. But too many rich people I know end up living financially *dependent* lives. Their choices are too often determined by the need to make more and more money. I notice that in our vacation spot on Martha's Vineyard, the wealthiest people tend to have the shortest vacations, because every day away from *their* work costs them more money than it costs the rest of us. When money enslaves rather than liberates, something is wrong.

8
Don't Risk What You Don't Have Enough of to Get More of What You Have Plenty Of

I was once asked if there was a common thread among the criminal defendants I have represented. Although each case is different and each client warrants individualized representation, I have discerned one thread that seems present in a great many of my cases — especially those involving the wealthy and the powerful. Each of these defendants has virtually unlimited quantities of some things, such as money, power or access to sex or power. They, like everyone else, also had limited quantities of other things, such as life, health, duration of career, reputation, time with family, etc. They got into trouble by putting at risk what they had limited amounts of in order to increase the quantities of those things they had unlimited amounts of. Even if they were innocent of the crimes they were eventually convicted of, they came close enough to the line to provoke prosecution. A wealthy, aging woman like Leona Helmsley had limited time with her dying husband and a limited life expectancy; yet (according to the government's evidence) she risked all that — and served several years in prison — to save a few dollars on taxes at a time when she was worth billions of dollars. The same could be said of many other of my wealthy clients. Mike Tyson had a limited number of years to earn money in the ring, but he placed those valuable and irreplaceable years at risk by going into a hotel room at 3 o'clock in the morning, alone with a woman he hardly knew, at a time in his life when women were falling all over themselves to have sex with him. (Some even wanted to have sex with him *while* he was in prison!)

This phenomenon has certainly been true of many public figures, ranging from President Clinton to Hugh Grant to Congressman Condit.

I'm certainly not suggesting that you engage in a Harvard Business School–type cost-benefit analysis over every personal decision in your life. I have also seen lives ruined by too calculating an assessment of how any risk-taking may impact on some ultimate, but uncertain, goal.

I remember how liberating it felt when I realized that I was among that select category of Americans who is "non-confirmable" — a Washington insider's term referring to someone who is too controversial ever to be confirmed by the Senate for any office. Though I was never particularly interested in holding any public office, it was a confirmation of my life choices. Some of my eminently confirmable friends, who will never be nominated, live their lives with their eyes on the Senate. Not a prescription for a full and happy life!

"It will go on your permanent record," my mother always warned, every time I considered doing something risky — like signing a petition to spare the Rosenbergs from execution. I'm glad I didn't listen, and I'm proud of most of the risks I've taken.

But the risks taken by some of my clients and some public figures are of a different order of magnitude and irrationality. Their reckless actions suggest that for some people, the risk itself produces the thrill. For others, getting close to — or going over — the line has long been a way of life, and since they were never previously caught, they don't understand that there *is* any risk. Yet others just never stop to think, as they edge closer and closer to the line. If you are going to get close to any important lines that might affect your life, do it consciously and calculate whether the risks are worth the benefits. Maybe they are. But for many of my clients, they weren't.

As I write these words, the case dominating the news involves a missing intern and the congressman who belatedly admitted having had an affair with her before she went missing. All the pundits are wondering out loud why he didn't learn the lesson of previous attempts by politicians to cover up their dirty laundry. "Cover-ups always backfire," observed one Washington insider. Of course, they do — *if* you're eventually caught. Everyone who had to admit to a tawdry affair *now* wishes he had done so earlier and not tried to cover it up. Just ask former president Clinton. The point that is missed by the Monday-morning quarterbacking is that most cover-ups work! We only learn about the few that don't. At the time that the malefactor has to decide whether to admit his salacious conduct, he believes that if he doesn't admit it, no one will ever learn the truth. That has been his experience and that of his colleagues. Just imagine how many congressional affairs we never learn about. The mindset of the malefactor is that he will never be caught. And statistically, he may well be right. Regrettable as it is, that is the reality. The few who get caught then seem so foolish for having taken a risk that in *retrospect* seems so unwarranted. But in *prospect* — before he was caught — the risk looked a lot more acceptable. To understand is not to condone, but to enlighten and perhaps to prevent making the same mistake others have made.

9
Is There an Absolute Morality?

So you want to do good. Don't we all? But when you become a lawyer, you have to define good differently than you did before. As a lawyer, you're someone else's representative. You're acting on their behalf. You're their spokesperson. You may not like the term, but you're their mouthpiece. You are they, only you are better educated and more articulate. So doing good often means doing good specifically for your client, not for the world at large, and certainly not for yourself.

Don't worry — you're not alone out there. The priest has a similar problem. Once he hears a confession, he can no longer do good by ordinary objective standards. If the penitent confesses to having killed someone and even feeling the urge to do it again, any decent person would immediately want to call the police and have this dangerous killer arrested. But a priest can't do that. He has undertaken a higher obligation of confidentiality. The priest's obligation of confidentiality far exceeds that of the lawyer. The lawyer can't disclose past crimes, but can call the police if his client tells him that he will commit a future crime. The priest can't even do that. He can try to talk the penitent out of it, threaten him with eternal damnation, but he can't blow the whistle. In one of my novels, *The Advocate's Devil*, I fictionalize a discussion I've actually had with a priest (abridged below):

> *"What if a priest learned information during a confession that led him to believe that the penitent was going to kill someone? Could he reveal it to prevent a murder?"*
>
> *"Hey, Abe, that's my favorite hypothetical. I always use it when I'm teaching new priests about the seal."*
>
> *"So what do you tell them?"*
>
> *"Under our rules, it's not even a close question. No way can a priest disclose it."*
>
> *"What can he do?"*
>
> *"Plead, cajole, threaten eternal damnation. Anything short of disclosure."*
>
> *"Do priests really stick to that rule?"*
>
> *"You bet they do. Look, Abe, in real life almost no one ever gets information about a future crime. Of course, it has happened, and we just don't tell."*
>
> * * *
>
> *"What would you have done, Stan, if you had a choice between saving lives and disclosing a confession?"*
>
> *"I know what would be the right thing to do."*

"What?"

"Preserve the seal."

"Even at the cost of human lives?"

"Abe, I know this is hard for laypeople to understand. Our job is to save souls, not lives. We have to leave it to others to save lives. If we were ever to breach the seal of the confessional, it would make it impossible for us to save souls, because no one would confess."

"Sounds like the kinds of arguments that lawyers make."

"Lawyers are not in the business of saving souls. They are in the business of saving lives."

"No, we're not — unfortunately. We're in the business of defending people charged with crimes. And if we break our 'seal,' no one will trust us. It's a very similar argument."

* * *

"I made a promise of confidentiality to my client. Are you telling me to break a solemn promise?"

"Saving a life is more sacred than keeping a promise — for a lawyer."

"Remember, you're a lawyer, too."

"Yes, I am. However, I don't take confession as a lawyer*. I take it as a priest. If someone told me something* as a lawyer*, not as a priest, which could save a life, I would disclose it."*

"Has that ever happened to you?"

"No. Nor have I ever been told anything, as a priest, that could save a human life."

"I wonder what you would really do if that ever happened? If you really could save a life by disclosing what you learned as a priest in confession? You seem like too good a person to sit idly by watching an innocent human being, whom you could save, die."

"I wonder, too. I hope my faith will never be tested," Father Maklowski said.

"Mine sure is being tested, and I feel like I'm failing the test."[1]

Some people might describe such ethics as situational. I prefer a different term: "role responsibility." When you take on certain roles in our society, you give up certain options. As a professor, I can't disclose the grade I gave a student, even if that student were to attack me viciously and I knew the revenge motive behind his attack. I am constrained by my role. In almost every job you take, there will be issues of confidentiality, and whenever there is an obligation of confidentiality, there is a potential conflict with personal morality. I once represented a former CIA agent who believed that his obligation to disclose improper conduct by his former employer transcended the confidentiality pledge he was forced to take as a condition of his employment. People who worked for the cigarette industry have made similar decisions. Most have complied with their pledge of confidentiality.

"How does it make you feel when you have to compromise your ethics by defending guilty criminals?" This is a question I am asked at least once a week. I once asked a priest if he was ever asked the priestly analogue to that question: "How does it make you feel when you have to compromise your ethics by not disclosing crimes that penitents confide to you during confession?" He was shocked: "What do you mean, 'compromise my ethics'? That *is* my ethic — not to disclose what I have been told in the confessional." He stated indignantly that he had *never* been asked that question or anything like it.

Most thoughtful people don't accept the criminal defense lawyer's answer to the original question: "What do you mean, 'compromise my ethics'? That *is* my ethic — to defend people accused of crime, whether I believe that they may be innocent or guilty." If you can't deal with that, don't become a defense lawyer.

10
Should Good Lawyers Defend Bad People?

A few years ago my wife was involved in a minor litigation. The controversy was sent to mediation where both sides were represented by excellent lawyers. The lawyer for the opposing side was anxious to settle the matter, since my wife was clearly in the right, both legally and morally. (We agreed to mediation only because litigation, which we would have won, would have been incredibly time-consuming and expensive.) I was at the mediation to lend support to my wife, who is a psychologist, not a lawyer. The opposing lawyer was, in my view, particularly nice and extremely polite, but he represented his client — a particularly sleazy enterprise — with vigor. At the first recess, my wife, who rarely has a negative word to say about anyone, was furious at the opposing lawyer. "How can he represent those people?" she fumed. "Doesn't he know he's on the wrong side? How does he sleep at night?"

As soon as she uttered that last rhetorical question, my wife smiled, realizing that she was saying all of the same things people say about me when I represent clients they believe are guilty, bad or wrong. Only after she won the case and got a nice settlement did she really calm down and appreciate that the opposing lawyer was doing his job. "I guess I'm equating him with his client," my wife said sheepishly. "That's what they always do to you."

Imagine a legal system in which lawyers were equated with the clients they defended and were condemned for representing controversial or despised defendants. Actually, one need not resort to imagination, since history reminds us that less than half a century ago, mainstream lawyers were frightened away from defending alleged communists who faced congressional witch hunts, blacklisting, criminal trials and even execution. Senator Joseph McCarthy and the millions of Americans — including many lawyers, law professors and bar association leaders — who supported this attack on "commie-symp lawyers" made it impossible for decent lawyers who despised communism but who supported civil liberties and constitutional rights for all to defend accused communists without risking their careers.

I grew up at the time Julius and Ethel Rosenberg were accused of being Soviet spies who gave the secret of the atomic bomb to our archenemies. They were defended by a communist ideologue with little experience in criminal cases. He provided an inept defense and the result was a terrible miscarriage of justice that has only recently been confirmed by Soviet intelligence sources. It now seems clear that the government framed Ethel Rosenberg in a futile effort to get her husband, who was a minor spy, to disclose the names of his accomplices (who were major spies). There is no assurance that an able and zealous mainstream lawyer could have saved either or both of the Rosenbergs from the electric chair, but we should certainly be left with an uncomfortable feeling that McCarthyite attacks on lawyers may well have contributed to a terrible injustice — and to some very bad law — in the *Rosenberg* and other cases during the 1940s and 1950s.

In many parts of the world, it remains difficult today for a despised defendant to be represented by a mainstream lawyer, because many nations — even Western-style democracies — lack any tradition of apolitical or civil libertarian representation. For example, in Israel, which has an excellent legal system, right-wing lawyers tend to represent right-wingers accused of political crimes, while left-wing lawyers tend to represent left-wingers and Palestinians accused of political crimes. (This situation has improved somewhat in recent years, thanks to a developing legal aid system.) This ideological approach to legal representation creates a circular reality in which lawyers are expected to share the political perspectives of their clients. The result is a bar divided along ideological lines that lacks a neutral commitment to civil liberties for all. A similar situation prevails in France, Italy and some other European countries.

Our nation has been blessed with the tradition of a vigorous bar committed to civil liberties for all, regardless of ideology, politics or the nature of the accusation. John Adams, Abraham Lincoln and Clarence Darrow have come to personify this approach. Adams represented the British soldiers who participated in the Boston Massacre; Lincoln and Darrow represented the widest assortment of clients, ranging from corporations to common criminals to the oppressed. It would be a terrible tragedy if we were to surrender this noble tradition to those who are so certain about their ability to discover truth that they become impatient with the often imperfect processes of justice. It was the great judge Learned Hand who once observed that "the spirit of liberty is the spirit that is not too sure that it is right."

It is a rare case in which absolute truth resides clearly on one side. Most cases contain shades of gray and are matters of degree. That has surely been true of most of the cases in which I have participated over my career. Even in those that are black and white — either the defendant did it or he did not — there is often room for disagreement, and it is the advocate's role to present the client's perspective zealously within the bounds of law and ethics. Zealous representation requires subordinating all other interests — ideological, career, personal — to the legitimate interest of the client. You are the surgeon in the operating room whose only goal is to save the patient, whether that patient is a good person or a bad person, a saint or a criminal. It is an extremely rare case in which a lawyer knows for sure that his client is guilty and that there are no mitigating considerations. In most of those cases the lawyer will try to persuade the defendant to enter into a plea bargain — not because that is best for society or the legal system, but because it is best for the client.

Having made this general point, it is important to suggest several distinctions among types of legal representation. At the pinnacle of cases that should be defended vigorously without regard to ideology are free speech and criminal matters. Surely those of us who defend the free speech rights of *everyone* — including extremists on the right and left, purveyors of sexual material and newspapers that make honest mistakes — should not be deemed to approve of the *content* of the materials the government seeks to censor. Those of us who opposed efforts by the town of Skokie to censor Nazis did not sympathize with the Nazis; we opposed censorship even of the most despicable and false ideas. It should be equally obvious that those of us who choose to defend people facing execution or long imprisonment do not sympathize with murder, rape, robbery or corporate crime. I personally despise criminals and always root for the good guys except when I am representing one of the bad guys. We believe in the process of American justice, which requires zealous advocacy, scrupulous compliance with constitutional safeguards and the rule of law. We understand that most people brought to trial for serious crimes are factually guilty. Thank goodness for that!

Would anyone want to live in a country in which the majority of criminal defendants were innocent? That may be true of Iran and Libya, but it is certainly not true of the United States. And in order to keep it that way, *every* defendant — regardless of his or her probability of guilt, unpopularity or poverty — must be vigorously defended within the rules of ethics. The scandal is not that the rich *are* zealously defended; it is that the poor and middle class are *not*. More resources should be allocated to defending those who cannot afford to challenge the prosecution and to expose the weaknesses of the evidence against them. There are indeed some innocent people in prison and on death row, and it is no coincidence that most of them are poor and unable to secure effective legal advocacy. That is why I devote half of my time to probono cases. Many other lawyers also do a significant amount of free legal representation, but this is not enough to ensure that no defendant faces execution or long imprisonment without zealous advocacy on his behalf. If lawyers are frightened away from taking on unpopular criminal cases, the already serious problem of inadequate representation will reach crisis proportions. There is no surer way of frightening a young lawyer who is contemplating the defense of an accused murderer or rapist than to accuse him or her of being sympathetic to murder or sexual abuse (as I was when I became part of the O.J. Simpson defense team).

Of course a lawyer has the legal and ethical option of declining to represent an unpopular and despised defendant whom he believes to be guilty. The real question is whether it is desirable for the decent lawyer to exercise that option on the basis of the "politically correct" criterion of the day, which differs from time to time. Today, it is popular to represent communists, because communism presents no threat, but it is unpopular to represent Islamic fundamentalists accused of terrorism. I believe no lawyer should turn down a constitutional or criminal case simply because the client or cause is deemed "politically incorrect" since — among other things — it will lead to the demise of civil liberties and to the creation of a bar so divided along ideological lines that the defendants who most need legal representation will be relegated to legal ideologues who often believe that politics and passion are a substitute for preparation and professionalism.

Several years ago, I got into a scrap with the Boston chapter of the Lawyers Guild, a left-wing group that deemed it politically incorrect to represent accused rapists. They changed their position only after an African-American man was accused of serially raping white women and the defendant claimed he was the victim of a racist misidentification.

Free speech and criminal cases are different from cases involving only continuing commercial gain from immoral conduct. A lawyer who provides ongoing legal assistance to a cocaine cartel is acting, in effect, as a "consigliere" to a criminal conspiracy. A criminal organization has no legal right to continuous advice on how to evade arrest and increase illegal profits. Many lawyers regard the cigarette industry as indistinguishable from the "mob" (though recent settlements suggest that even cigarette lawyers can sometimes help their clients do the right thing, if only for self-serving reasons). Corporations that are not facing criminal charges do not have the same Sixth Amendment rights as accused criminals, nor do they have the same First Amendment rights as those confronting government censorship. Still, we are all better off with a legal system under which important rights are not denied anyone without affording them the right to be defended by a zealous advocate. If we move away from the American tradition of lawyers defending those with whom they vehemently disagree — as we temporarily did during the McCarthy period — we weaken our commitment to the rule of law. What is popular today may be despised tomorrow. So beware of an approach that limits advocacy to that which is approved by the standards of political correctness.

A recent case in Massachusetts places limits on a lawyer's discretion to decline a case. A feminist attorney who specializes in representing women in divorce cases refused to represent a male nurse's aide who was seeking financial support from his wealthy wife who was a doctor. The lawyer told the man that she did not accept male clients in divorce cases. A panel of the Massachusetts Commission Against Discrimination ruled against the lawyer, stating "that an attorney [holding herself] out as open to the public may not reject a potential client solely on the basis of gender or some other protected class." Obviously this situation is different from one in which a lawyer declines a case on political or ideological grounds, but it does suggest that lawyers are not entirely free to decline cases on *any* ground. In selecting clients, a lawyer may be a feminist but not a sexist. The distinction may be subtle, but it is real. Lawyers in Massachusetts, as in other states, are covered by civil rights and public accommodation laws, some of which prohibit discrimination based on religion, creed and political affiliation. Doctors and dentists are not free to turn away patients who had AIDS or whose politics they despise. It is a fair question to ask why lawyers should have greater freedom to discriminate than do other professionals.

In the end, I hope lawyers will not need laws to tell them that they should represent those most in need of zealous advocacy, without regard to gender, race, ideology, economic situation or popularity. Such an approach will make for a better legal system and a freer America.

The one thing a lawyer is never free to do is to accept a case and then pursue it without zeal. Although there are no specific criteria for measuring zeal, there certainly are general guidelines. As I will explain later, being someone's lawyer is different from being their friend. For a friend or relative, you may be willing to sacrifice your life, your liberty or your fortune. You need not — and should not — do that for a client, even a client you like. Zealous advocacy has limits imposed by law, ethics and common sense. We know what unzealous representation means: Just look at some of the capital case lawyers in Texas! Several fell asleep during trial. Others conducted no investigation. Many judges prefer underzealous to overzealous lawyers. That's why they appoint the former — who make their job easier, if they define their job as sentencing as many defendants as possible to death. Overzealous lawyers are a pain in the ass to some judges. I know. I am one. We make their job harder by contesting every issue, demanding every right and disputing every prosecutorial allegation, so long as it is in the best interest of the client (both short-term and long-term). That is the key to defining appropriately zealous advocacy: It must always be in the legitimate interest of the client. Its purpose is not to make you feel good or virtuous, but to help the client win by any ethical and lawful means.

11 Defending Yourself from Legal McCarthyism

In the aftermath of the O.J. Simpson case, I was subjected, along with the other members of the defense team, to vicious attacks by talk-show hosts, editorial writers and even some lawyers. I responded to many of these attacks. I am reprinting two of my responses here, because they amplify points in the previous chapter and may provide some implicit advice about how to respond to the inevitable attacks you will receive if you become a criminal defense lawyer. The first response was to an article by Laurie Levenson, an associate dean at Loyola law school and a former prosecutor who served as a paid TV commentator on the Simpson case. The second response was to Professor Peter Gabel, who wrote an article criticizing defense lawyers who represent guilty defendants.

Some lawyers, too young to remember the lessons of McCarthyism, have tried to repeat them.

Dean Laurie Levinson has apparently not learned the lessons of the Rosenberg tragedy or of the McCarthyism that led to it. In her screed against defense lawyers, she makes essentially the same argument that Senator McCarthy made. She chastises me for representing O. J. Simpson, who was facing the death penalty at the time I joined his defense team. She argues that in helping to defend Simpson — and other men whom she does not like — I am not "improving the world" or defending "a good cause." She seems to have little understanding of the adversary system or the role of zealous counsel. She calls the defendant's right to representation a "cloak" and a "game." Perhaps she would understand its importance if she had spent ten years, as I did, representing Soviet refuseniks on a pro bono basis in a society which denied them the right to effective representation. I do not recall Levinson volunteering her time to causes she deems righteous. Instead she has exploited the Simpson case for her own self-aggrandizement.

If Levinson's views were ever to become accepted, it would become difficult to secure counsel for unpopular defendants deemed guilty by the public. Because I have tenure, I can resist Levinson's vicious attacks on my motives and integrity. Imagine a young lawyer just out of law school needing to endure such attacks from a law school dean as a consequence of representing someone of whom she disapproves.

If Levinson's self-righteous criteria were to be accepted, then no decent lawyer would represent Oklahoma bomber Timothy McVeigh, Mikhail Markhasev (the man accused of killing Ennis Cosby), accused Nazi war criminal John Demjanjuk or the Rosenbergs. It is no answer to say that "others" should do it. No lawyer asked to represent a defendant facing the death penalty should decline. The problem is not with lawyers who agree to take such cases. It is with those like Laurie Levinson, who don't.

When a rabbi recently asked me to consult on a case involving a Jewish man on death row, should I have sought Levinson's permission first? Should I have determined, before taking the case, whether Levinson believes that it was a "good cause" which would "improve the world?"

Perhaps if Levinson was familiar with the traditional Jewish sources, she would know that a Sanhedrin that was unanimous in condemning a man to death could not order his execution, since unanimity meant that the defendant lacked a zealous advocate within the tribunal. The Torah and the Talmud understood advocacy, even if Levinson does not.

I have been thinking, teaching, writing about these issues a good many years. Three of my books deal explicitly with the ethical issues of a defense lawyer representing defendants who may well be guilty.[1]

Levinson certainly has the right to disagree with me on the merits of my cases or clients, but her ad hominem attack on my personal integrity is beneath contempt. Lawyers and philosophers have been debating these complex issues since Abraham argued with God about the people of Sodom. Levinson's pathetic attempt to pander to the public by reducing these complexities to simple-minded issues of gamesmanship insults the intelligence of all who care about balancing individual rights against effective law enforcement.

Dear Editor:

There are few more dangerous ideologues than those who believe that truth can be arrived at without process. You would have thought that Professor Peter Gabel might have learned that lesson from both communism and Nazism which adopted procedures closely akin to the one he proposes. Those who burned witches and conducted inquisitions also believed that they were serving "the well-being of the wider community and the creation of a more human and just society." Gabel's road may be paved with good intentions but it will surely lead to hell.

Gabel says, "In cases where the client is charged with committing acts of brutality or cruelty, neither the presumption of innocence nor the rights to counsel justifies an effort to obtain a verdict of not guilty if the lawyer does not believe his or her client is in fact innocent." Indeed he goes further and says that, "the moral situation is not changed significantly when you strongly suspect or even believe that your client is guilty of such conduct." This approach virtually abolishes the role of defense counsel and turns every "defense" lawyer into a prosecutor and judge whose job it is to "suspect" his or her client and treat the client as guilty based on mere suspicion.

To illustrate the naïve nature of this simple-minded approach, I challenge Professor Gabel to respond to the following questions:

1. *Assume a system in which the Exclusionary role — either under the Fourth or Fifth Amendments — continues to exist. Assume that you have been appointed to represent a woman facing the death penalty for killing her abusive husband. Assume that the police broke into the defendant's home without a warrant and discovered evidence suggesting that the murder was planned. Would Gabel preclude the woman's appointed lawyer from invoking the Fourth or Fifth Amendment so as to exclude this evidence? Would Gabel also deny the lawyer the right to object to hearsay testimony in cases where the lawyer suspected that his or her client may be guilty?*
2. *Assume the same case. Would the appointed lawyer be obliged to tell his client in advance that*

whatever the client told him would not be kept confidential and that if the client told him anything incriminating the lawyers would no longer vigorously defend the client? Would that not simply result in clients never telling their lawyers anything of an incriminating nature?

3. *Would lawyers who adopt the Gabel approach, as distinguished from the civil liberties approach, have to identify themselves as Gabel lawyers, rather than as defense lawyers? If so, can you imagine any reason why a defendant who might suspect that this lawyer might believe him guilty, would ever go to a Gabel lawyer?*
4. *Does Gabel concede that under the current constitutional and ethical rules, a defense lawyer who suspects or believes that his client may be guilty and who refrains from invoking all ethically available legal and constitutional defenses — such as the exclusionary rule — would be violating both the Sixth Amendment and the ethical requirements of the legal profession? (If he does not, he should read* DeLuca v. Lord, *77 F.3d 578.)*
5. *If Gabel does concede this, does it not follow that accusing a defense lawyer who complies with his obligation to current law of having "his hand still dripping from the blood of the victims whose assassins he protected"*[2] *reeks of blatant McCarthyism and fails to understand the constitutional obligation of defense counsel under current law?*

Arriving at truth in a system committed to civil liberties is a complex phenomenon. Gabel's simple-minded solutions will move us back to the dark ages where truth could be found by the rack and the Star Chamber.[3]

12
How to Balance Idealism, Realism and Cynicism

Oliver Wendell Holmes, Jr., was one of the great cynics in legal history. Once, when an idealistic law clerk challenged an opinion the justice had written, accusing him of producing a result that was unjust, the old man replied, "We are in the law business, not the justice business." Many young people go into the practice of law hoping to live a life of justice.

The *Deuteronomy* book of the Bible commands, "Justice, justice shall you pursue." When asked why the word "justice" is repeated, one ancient commentator replied that there are two aspects of justice: the *end* of convicting only the guilty, and the *means* that requires that in the interest of rarely convicting the innocent, we sometimes acquit the guilty. It is not long before the young lawyer realizes that no one really wants justice. Everyone wants to win. The façade behind which the desire to win is hidden is called justice. Sometimes an honest litigant acknowledges his real goal, as in the story of the lawyer who e-mails his client, "Justice has prevailed." The client immediately e-mails his response: "Appeal immediately."

Some lawyers cannot tolerate playing a role in the justice system that requires them to produce unjust results. They seek a role that permits them to pursue pure justice: becoming a prosecutor or a judge or an academic. Surely, without the need to represent individual clients, one can seek pure justice. Well, maybe. But in my experience, most don't. They still want to win. They may define winning differently, but the goal is still going to be the same. I have never met a prosecutor who didn't want to win. They persuade themselves, of course, that by winning, they are achieving justice, since they would never knowingly prosecute an innocent person, but winning is also the key to promotion and the criteria by which success is measured.

It may sound surprising to some, but most judges, too, want to win. They want to win the acclaim of their peers. They, too, want to be promoted. Every judge, other than the Chief Justice of the United States, has a secret desire to rise even higher within the judiciary. Even if some realize that they will never make it to the Supreme Court, they want their decisions studied in law school, reported favorably in the media or praised by their colleagues. That, too, is winning, since it sometimes places personal interests before considerations of abstract justice.

This is particularly true in the United States, where prosecutors and judges are political. They are either elected or appointed by politicians (and subject to confirmation by other politicians). We are the only country in the Western world that has so politicized our system of justice. The result is that we have no real system of justice. We have yet another political branch of government whose results are measured by political considerations. The only institution in our legal system that ever tries to do pure individual justice is the jury. It doesn't always succeed. But since a jury can have no career ambition — it disappears as an entity upon completion of its singular task and its members go back to their ordinary lives — it can focus exclusively on doing the right thing. Now even that process has been corrupted somewhat in high-profile cases, by the prospect of book deals, TV interviews and even rewards by some litigants.

Welcome to the real world. How are you going to deal with it? Every lawyer must be a legal realist. (What's the alternative? A legal pretender or "fakist"?) A lawyer is paid for his or her insights into how the legal system really works, and politics, ambition and other personal factors play important roles in how cases are actually decided. In the old days, judges wore wigs to make them all look alike (the fact that they were all white males helped too). Today in our country, they still wear robes, which are essentially uniforms — despite Chief Justice Rehnquist's need to individuate himself by sporting Gilbert and Sullivan stripes on his robe. But the uniformity of the robes does nothing to hide the great differences among judges and the nonuniformity of the way different judges would decide the same case. Until fairly recently, the Code of Judicial Conduct frowned on dissenting opinions, which were thought to diminish the grandeur of the courts.

There is a place for idealism in this world of winner-take-all, but idealism must be filtered through the lens of realism, lest you become naïve. There is even room for constructive cynicism, but it, too, must be balanced against idealism and realism. An unrealistic cynic is as naïve as an unrealistic idealist, just a lot less noble.

13 Your Last Exam

You may think you took your last exam when you passed the bar, but the legal profession is a never-ending series of exams that are graded by judges, juries, senior partners, clients and others. The grading system is generally "pass-fail," but unlike in those colleges and law schools that employ the pass-fail system, in the real-life tests, "fail" is a common grade. You will lose cases, clients and face with some regularity, no matter how good you are — or think you are. Law, unlike school, is often a zero-sum game that is not graded on a curve. Moreover, there is no necessary correlation between the quality of your work and whether you pass or fail. You will lose cases in which you have done a far better job than your opponent, because your opponent has the better or easier side, or because the judge or jury is inclined in favor of his or her client. You are not alone in this respect. Although doctors don't face judges or juries (unless they are accused of malpractice), some of the best performed operations end up with a dead patient and some of the worst with merely an ugly scar. Much depends on factors beyond the control of the doctor, just as much depends on matters beyond the control of the lawyer. Of course, a good doctor or lawyer factors these unknowable but ever-present risks into the calculation of whether or not to operate or litigate, but even a correct decision to proceed, and the most technically proficient operation or litigation, may produce disaster for the patient or client.

It is essential that professionals who are judged by others develop internal criteria for self-evaluation of their work product. I have tried to do that over the course of my professional life. I'm very tough on myself, even when I win — indeed, especially when I win, because no one else is critical then (except if I win a case for an extremely unpopular client, but even then the nature of the criticism is different). It began as a law student, when I received an A in my third-year property exam that I knew I did not deserve. I actually told the professor that I thought he was overly generous to me. He agreed, telling me that since I was the highest-ranking student in the third-year class and he was a new assistant professor, he feared that giving me the B or B+ we both knew I deserved would — I remember his words to this day — "reflect more poorly on me than on you." I have always thought of my "real" grade in that course as a B rather than an A and rationalized my inflated actual grade as a makeup for the C I got in contracts, which was lower than I thought I deserved.

I recall one incident a few years later that confirmed my view of the legal profession as a lifelong series of exams by often inaccurate graders. I worked on a complex criminal case with a retired federal judge who had recently left the bench to accept a partnership with a major law firm. He lost his first case, and he lost it badly, despite his best efforts. He never tried another case, preferring instead to do transaction work. When I asked him why he had given up on trials, which he loved, and moved to an area that bored him, he replied, "I'm too old to be tested. I'm ready for a job where everyone wins."

There are such win-win jobs in the legal profession, but not in litigation. So if you're not prepared for a life of being tested and graded by others often less competent than you are, pick a win-win area of the law. Prepare wills. Dead clients don't grade you!

14 Self-Doubts

I was fifteen years old before anyone told me I was smart. I was a very poor student — both academically and disciplinarily — in both elementary and high school. I cared more about sports, girls and jokes than I did about arithmetic or Talmud (I went to a yeshiva). Neither of my parents had gone to college and I thought I would end up selling clothing, like my father. I didn't see how history or spelling would make me a better salesman, but scoring a basket, getting a good laugh or flirting with a girl provided immediate gratification. My grades were generally in the C range (except for penmanship, at which I excelled, and deportment, where my grades hovered between D's and F's). The only encouraging sign was that I generally got F's in "effort," which subtly suggested that at least some teachers believed I might be able to do better if I tried harder. But if they believed this, they never told me, except my eighth grade teacher, Mr. Kien, who had also been my father's teacher thirty years earlier. He once told me that my father hadn't been much of a student and he turned out fine. Although Mr. Kien later told me that he had intended this observation to be taken as encouragement, that's not the way I understood it, since my father had never become a good student.

But Yitz Greenberg, the first person who told me I was smart, didn't beat around the bush. He was the dramatics counselor at Camp Eton, where I worked as a waiter between my junior and senior years in high school. By that time I had become — in my own mind, at least — a somewhat more serious student, but I had such a bad reputation in high school that my teachers refused to take me seriously. In fact, when I got a grade of 100 on my statewide physics regent, the teacher accused me of cheating. His accusation was corroborated when I won a state scholarship on the basis of a competitive statewide exam. Only after determining that I sat behind the dumbest kid in the school and next to no one else who did well on the exam was I acquitted of the false charges.

Yitz didn't need to see my exam scores. We had long conversations about religion, philosophy, literature, drama and — of course — girls. One day he just blurted it out: "You know, you're really smart." I know he meant it, because he wasn't the flattering type and, anyway, why would he need to flatter me? His statement changed my life. It gave me the confidence to act as if I were smart, despite my lingering doubts.

As soon as I changed schools — from Yeshiva High School to Brooklyn College — I blossomed academically. My reputation did not follow me to my large public college, so I could start from scratch. My ambition to become a lawyer, which I had harbored secretly for several years, seemed achievable and I loved learning from professors with open minds. I don't remember getting very many B's in my life. I went from being a C student to an A student.

I later learned that everyone has lingering doubts, regardless of how many A's they get or how much praise they receive from teachers. Deep down we all know our own weaknesses better than anyone else, and we think everyone else knows them too. Self-doubt is a powerful motivator, so long as it doesn't become unrealistic. Then it can immobilize.

15

The Perfect Is the Enemy of the Excellent

When I arrived at Harvard Law School in 1964, there were several extremely distinguished professors who rarely wrote anything. Their reputations for brilliance were so high and so universal that they had nowhere to go but down. They feared — correctly, I suspect — that if they published widely, criticism would begin to emerge. So they limited their published output to the occasional "perfect gem," which they had polished for years. Other works were circulated as "preliminary drafts" or "works in progress," so as to preclude reviews or other criticism. The great fear was that their "perfect" reputations might be tarnished by a less-than-perfect piece of writing.

After several years on the faculty, I came to realize that their need for perfection had deterred them from publishing excellent, if imperfect, works. I also realized that there is no such thing as a perfect piece of work.

Every book, painting, symphony or speech could be improved. The search for perfection is illusory and has no end.

It was then that I began to publish my many imperfect books. The result has been personally very satisfying, though my writings have, of course, been subject to criticism, much of it warranted.

Today I write nearly every day and publish a book almost every year. I feel the need to share my ideas as widely as possible. Having spent so many years taking in information, I feel the need to get out as much as possible. My test for publication is certainly not perfection. Instead, I ask myself whether sharing my experiences, mistakes, insights and opinions will contribute in a positive way to the marketplace of ideas. I see the publication of my ideas as part of a teaching and learning process. I learn from the criticism directed at my writings. I teach by putting out my ideas, without subjecting them first to endless honing, polishing and internal peer review. The marketplace of ideas will hone, polish and review. So don't hold back until it's perfect. Get it out. And don't become one of those people who has to show every draft to a hundred friends and colleagues before letting go. The resulting product may be more "sound" and less subject to criticism, but it will also be less distinctive — more theirs, and in the end less yours. Have confidence in your own writing.

16
An Honorable Profession?

So you think you've entered an honorable profession! You've heard Law Day speeches about the rule of law. You've seen the slogans on the side of courthouses proclaiming equal justice under law. You've heard judges raise their hand to God and swear that they will do justice without "respect to persons." Now welcome to the real world. As a lawyer, you will see corruption all around you, unless you deliberately blind yourself to it. You will hear policemen lying through their teeth to convict people who they believe are guilty but whose constitutional rights they violated in order to secure the evidence of their guilt. You will see judges who know these policemen are lying, pretending to believe them in order to avoid freeing an obviously guilty defendant. You will read the opinions of court of appeals judges pretending to believe the trial judges who pretended to believe the police who pretended to be telling the truth. This sort of "benign" corruption is pervasive in our legal system — and everyone with any experience knows it. Yet we hear nothing about it on Law Day. We never see the slogan that should adorn every courthouse: "The end justifies the means." Nor do we hear judges take the oath they really follow: "to do justice without respect to person" — unless those persons are drug dealers, Mafioso or represented by lawyers we don't like.

Nearly twenty years ago, I conceived what I called the thirteen Rules of the Criminal Justice Game. Most of the participants in the criminal justice system understand them. Although these rules never appear in judicial opinions, they seem to control the realities of the process. Like all rules, they are necessarily stated in oversimplified terms. But they tell an important part of how the system operates in practice. Here are some of the key rules of the justice game:

Rule I Most criminal defendants are, in fact, guilty.

Rule II All criminal defense lawyers, prosecutors and judges understand and believe Rule I.

Rule III It is easier to convict guilty defendants by violating the Constitution than by complying with it, and in some cases it is impossible to convict guilty defendants without violating the Constitution.

Rule IV Many police lie about whether they violated the Constitution in order to convict guilty defendants.

Rule V	All prosecutors, judges and defense attorneys are aware of Rule IV.
Rule VI	Many prosecutors implicitly encourage police to lie about whether they violated the Constitution in order to convict guilty defendants.
Rule VII	All judges are aware of Rule VI.
Rule VIII	Most trial judges pretend to believe police officers who they know are lying.
Rule IX	All appellate judges are aware of Rule VIII, yet many pretend to believe the trial judges who pretend to believe the lying police officers.
Rule X	Most judges disbelieve defendants about whether their constitutional rights have been violated, even if they are telling the truth.
Rule XI	Most judges and prosecutors would not knowingly convict a defendant who they believe to be innocent of the crime charged (or a closely related crime).
Rule XII	Rule XI does not apply to members or organized crime, drug dealers, career criminals or potential informers.
Rule XIII	Nobody really wants justice.

Benign corruption has, if anything, gotten worse in the past twenty years, as courts blind themselves to the reality of how the system really works.

You will also see malignant corruption. You will meet partners who overbill their clients. Other partners have drinks with judges and then tell clients they have these judges in their pocket. You will meet clients who can't tell the difference between the truth and a lie, except that they have far more practice with the latter than with the former.

None of this should really come as a surprise to you if you've been paying close attention to what you read in law school. The rot always starts from the head down, and if you have carefully read Supreme Court decisions, you will have seen plenty of corruption. And I'm not talking only about *Bush v. Gore*. I'm referring to the many cases in which Supreme Court justices distort the record, twist the law and engage in conduct that, if they were ordinary lawyers, would subject them to discipline.[1] If you become a law clerk, you'll see it with your own eyes. In fact, you'll probably become part of it, unless you decide — in advance — that you will not become complicit in this system of elite cheating that is so prevalent in our legal system.

17
Blowing the Whistle[1]

What should a law clerk do if he or she were to have observed any improprieties by a judge or justice? Consider the recent election case. Would a law clerk who saw corruption be ethically obliged to come forward and disclose it? These are questions I have posed — in the abstract — for years in my third-year legal ethics course at Harvard Law School. Many of my students have gone on to serve as Supreme Court law clerks, and I wonder if any are now facing such questions in the concrete context of this case.

Law clerks do have confidential relationships with their justices, but does this confidentiality transcend their duty to the public? Law clerks, like lawyers who serve in the White House Counsel's office, work for the United States government. Their loyalty runs, as a matter of law, to the institution of the Supreme Court, not to the individual justices in whose chambers they work.

Obviously, they should not tell journalists about the entirely lawful inner workings of the High Court. But if they have been privy to any improprieties — ethical or legal — their primary obligation is to disclose such improprieties to the proper authorities.

Under our system of separation of powers, it is not clear who the proper authorities would be if a law clerk felt bound to report a judicial impropriety. The judiciary claims the power to self-regulate. Complaints about lower federal judges are supposed to be directed to the Judicial Conference, which is comprised of other federal judges. But the Supreme Court has exempted itself from the jurisdiction of this body. As such, the justices have placed themselves above the very law they purport to administer. If the violation were criminal — say, for example, the taking of a bribe — the law clerk could go to federal prosecutors. But most judicial misconduct does not rise to the level of reportable criminal behavior.

I am aware of no evidence of any criminal conduct in this or any other Supreme Court case. But there is evidence of a disqualifying conflict of interest by at least one of the majority justices. According to press reports, Justice Sandra Day O'Connor expressed distress over the possibility that Gore might win the election. "This is terrible," she reportedly said upon hearing initial news reports that Gore had carried Florida. She and her husband have reportedly discussed with friends her strong desire to retire from the Supreme Court and return to Arizona. They have told friends, however, that she would not do so unless Bush were elected President and could replace her with another Republican. If this is true, then the heavy thumb of material advantage was placed on the scale of her judgment in the election case. She should have recused herself, because she had expressed the wish for a particular outcome — an outcome that she helped to bring about. There was not only an appearance of impropriety but also the reality that the outcome she voted for as a justice would facilitate her retirement plans. If a law clerk were privy to any conversation that confirmed this impropriety, he or she would be ethically obliged to disclose it. But the question remains: To whom should the disclosure be made?

The Supreme Court has ruled, in two other cases involving the Presidency — the Nixon tapes case and the Clinton–Paula Jones case — that no person or institution is above the law in America. But these same justices have placed themselves and the Supreme Court above the law. Now that they have jumped feet-first into the thicket of partisan politics, there is no conceivable justification for their special status. If Justice O'Connor violated the code of judicial conduct by participating in a case whose outcome would materially affect her retirement plans, she should be disciplined, in the way that other judges have been disciplined for participating in cases in which they or the families may have had a material interest. The same is true for any other justice who may have violated the rules by their participation in the election case. For example, if any justice instructed a law clerk to find a legal justification for ruling in favor of a particular candidate, this would be improper. We can only learn of any such possible improprieties, if they indeed occurred, from insiders.

Will a conscience-stricken law clerk now come forward and blow the whistle, if there is indeed any cause in this case for whistle-blowing? Judicial historians will almost certainly discover someday what went on behind the scenes of the High Court's result-oriented decision in the election case. There may well be tarnished reputations, not only of justices but also of law clerks who may have known but who remained silent. This may be the time for good men and women to speak up.

18 The Good, the Bad, the Honest and the Dishonest

What makes a good lawyer? About once a day I'm asked to recommend a "good lawyer" to someone. Often I can come up with the name of someone appropriate with whom I have actually worked or whose work I have observed close up. Sometimes he was my co-counsel or opponent. Other times I may have read the trial transcript of a case in which she was lead counsel. But for many lawyers, all I have to go on is their reputation, and that can be more a product of careful public relations than of proven excellence. I have seen lawyers with great reputations come into court unprepared and do terrible jobs.

I take recommendations very seriously, in part because many of my own cases come to me through the recommendations of lawyers with whom I have worked or who have seen my work. (My favorite recommendation, however, came from a prison inmate whose appeal I had lost but who thought I had done a good job.)

The best I can do in recommending someone whose work I have not personally seen is to speak frankly to the person I am recommending and tell him or her that I am putting my own credibility on the line by my recommendation and that I intend to follow the case by reviewing the lawyer's work products — briefs, motions, etc. That way, I at least provide some assurance that the lawyer will take the case seriously and do the required preparation and if he doesn't, I can tell the client and be sure not to recommend the lawyer again.

Beyond that, I can generally provide some assurance that the lawyer will be honest. And then I have to explain what "honest" means in the context of our often dishonest legal system.

Several years ago I received a phone call from a desperate mother in the Midwest whose son was facing a long prison term for triple manslaughter. She said that her son's lawyer had asked for $11,000 — in addition to his fee — to "wine and dine" the judge and prosecutor in order to get a shorter sentence for the son. Was the lawyer being "honest," the woman asked me — that is, was he really going to give the money to the judge and prosecutor and get the shorter sentence? Or was he going to be "dishonest" by keeping it for himself and getting nothing for his client?

I told the woman that the law had reached a pretty sorry state when an "honest" lawyer is defined as one who will actually keep his promise to pay a bribe. I advised her not to pay the money and urged her to report the lawyer to the proper law enforcement authorities. The mother ended our conversation by posing a question I am asked all the time: "Are there any honest lawyers left?"

The answer is an unequivocal *yes*. But they are sometimes hard to find among the thousands of dishonest, shady and disreputable lawyers who practice throughout this country. There is hardly a city or town in America where an ordinary citizen could safely pick an honest lawyer out of the Yellow Pages. Nor is corruption among lawyers limited to the local level, as evidenced by the large number of attorneys convicted of serious crimes in highly publicized national cases ranging from Watergate to Abscam to Iran-Contra to the conviction of former deputy attorney general Webb Hubble for cheating his clients. It has gotten so bad that I begin my first-year criminal law class at Harvard by telling the students that "statistically, it is likely that more of you will become criminal *defendants* than criminal defense *lawyers*."

Thousands of lawyers are publicly disciplined each year by the courts for various improprieties. This may be just the tip of the iceberg, since many clients don't even know they were being ripped off by their own lawyers, and some who do are too frightened to complain — especially since they would have to complain to other lawyers. Nonetheless, nearly one out of every ten attorneys in America faces malpractice claims from dissatisfied clients. Further, the number of informal admonitions and private reprimands far exceeds the number of public, court-imposed disciplinary procedures.

A subtle aura of corruption — or at least corruptibility — permeates the American legal system.

The legal profession is, to a large degree, responsible for this state of affairs, for it speaks to its initiates with a forked tongue: It preaches honesty, but all too often it practices and rewards corruption. There is widespread suspicion that some bar associations — which generally are responsible for overseeing lawyers — are not vigorous in pursuing corruption among fellow lawyers. This is particularly true of borderline corruption, such as influence-peddling, which is widely practiced by the kinds of lawyers active in bar associations.

Even honest lawyers are always bragging about whom they know, which helps perpetuate the view that the best lawyers are those who know the most judges. The subtle line between being "friendly" with a judge and actually "getting to him" in some way is often lost on the client. Why, after all, would a lawyer bother to mention his friendship with the judge unless that friendship could somehow help the client? As a result, the client will naturally seek out the influential lawyer, believing he can produce the best results. The client also will be charged accordingly.

Law schools must share the blame too. Their graduates are not adequately trained to confront the real-life temptations they are likely to encounter in the competitive world of law firms and clients. For many years, legal ethics has been the poor relation of American legal education. Professors Andrew Kaufman and Monroe Freedman — both experts in legal ethics — once debated the subject in my criminal law class. Kaufman noted that since they both had graduated from Harvard Law School, they had each learned legal ethics in the same place — on the street. And the street teaches that corruption is often rewarded by success, and playing by the theoretical rules is often punished by bankruptcy.

Following the embarrassment of Watergate (which might appropriately have been called "Lawyergate," since so many members of the bar were involved), this changed somewhat. The American Bar Association now insists that all law students take a course in legal ethics before graduating. But many of the resulting courses hold little promise of improving the situation. Students are told to be ethical, but they learn by example, not by moralistic pronouncements. Once they graduate, they continue to see the influence-peddlers and glad-handers rewarded and honored by their peers and clients. This generates cynicism and frustration even among the best and brightest young lawyers.

The temptations to get clients at any cost are likely to increase as more law school graduates compete for a relatively fixed number of law-related jobs.

Of course, the ultimate victim of lawyer corruption is the client — the consumer of justice. He often gets precious little for his money when he pays high fees for his lawyer's influence.

Yet, it is possible for the cycle to be broken. Consumers can protect themselves from unscrupulous lawyers. But first, the client must believe that an honest lawyer has a better chance of winning a case than a dishonest one. Few will believe it unless it becomes true.

How can you tell an honest lawyer from a dishonest one? There is no litmus test, but here are a few guidelines:

- Beware the lawyer who promises too much. Many dishonest lawyers are con artists and smooth talkers.
- Most lawyers who promise to use their influence are bluffing.
- To be sure, there are some situations where the lawyers can actually "fix" a case — where his friendship, influence or outright bribery can affect the outcome of the litigation. Those are the most outrageous and damaging cases of all and the judges involved are the real villains, because without them the entire charade would be exposed.
- Be suspicious of the lawyer who sells himself to you by downgrading other lawyers who are hard workers. "That guy may be good in the library," he says, "but the judges don't like him." This type of lawyer is generally short on legal abilities and spends his time at lawyer-judge luncheons, bar association cocktail parties and judicial conferences where he can be seen with the judges. That may help him, but not you! Many judges I

know are suspicious of the glad-handers and respect the hardworking lawyer who makes the judge's job easier by presenting the legal and factual arguments in a well-prepared manner.

- Always go for the lawyer who talks intelligently about legal and factual issues. Most cases — particularly small ones not involving politicized issues — really are decided on their merits and on the legal abilities of the lawyers.

A previous client once called to tell me that he had been approached by a lawyer to pay a bribe in order to obtain a lucrative municipal school busing contract to which he felt entitled. I went to the U.S. Attorney's office and told them the story. My client agreed to cooperate in a plan to catch the lawyer. It worked. The crooked lawyer was caught and sentenced to prison. My client got the contract. That story had a happy ending. But there are few happy endings for those clients who are led, by their lawyers, into bribery and corruption.

The framers of our Constitution — aided by judicial giants such as John Marshall, Oliver Wendell Holmes and Louis Brandeis — created a legal system designed to withstand the human frailties of lawyers and judges. The system will survive the corruption of its participants. But the key to achieving individual justice in a particular case is to find an able and honest lawyer. The next task facing the legal profession is to make it easier for the ordinary citizen to tell the difference between the honest lawyer and the shyster. For that to occur, there must be honest peer review and published evaluations of lawyers. Today, there are a few books available that contain peer reviews of lawyers in specific areas of practice. It is a beginning, but more needs to be done.

19
Your Client Is Not Your Friend

Your client is not your friend, and your friend should not become your client. There are cell blocks full of lawyers who made the mistake of believing that the charming rogue who paid a large fee and paid for expensive dinners was becoming his bosom buddy. Then the bosom buddy is convicted of a crime and produces a "get out of jail free" card. Lo and behold! It has your face on it. He's trading your freedom for his. In exchange for testifying against you, the prosecutor is willing to set him free. After all, you're the big-shot lawyer, and he's a nobody. The first rule for escaping prison in the United States is always having someone more important than yourself to incriminate. Your erstwhile client-friend understands that rule and knows you're that more important person.

But what can he say to incriminate you? Nothing, if you don't cross the line from lawyer to friend. Plenty, if you do cross that rubicon. After all, friends do things for friends that no lawyer should ever consider doing for a client. It may be as innocent-seeming as lighting up a joint. Or it may be as unethical as helping him "improve" his testimony. A lawyer was recently sentenced to ten years in federal prison for suborning perjury by allegedly assisting a client-friend in formulating a defense to drug charges.

When I was a young lawyer, I worked on an appeal for a wealthy, suave man-about-town. He was a bachelor who lived with his mother, but maintained a small pied-à-terre in midtown Manhattan, which he offered to his friends and lawyers for extramarital flings. Fortunately, I had no need for such an apartment. I later learned that he had installed a video camera that recorded these flings and gave the client the ammunition with which to blackmail his lawyer-friends. I have heard similar stories about lawyers being blackmailed by client-friends with whom they smoked pot, snorted cocaine or committed other vices and crimes.

Several years after I represented the client with the video camera, I argued an appeal on behalf of another client who paid me with a bounced check. He offered to replace the bad check with cash, insisting that I wouldn't have to report the cash on my income tax (as he had not on his). I told him that I report everything, and he looked at me like I was crazy. "Most of the lawyers I deal with," he said, "prefer cash because they don't report it." Although it is legal to accept cash fees,[1] I strongly recommend against it. Cash should always be a red flag. Why should anyone want to pay you in cash, unless *they* weren't reporting their income, or they want to have something to hold over you? I have a standard speech for clients who want to pay me in cash: "I can't be both your banker and your lawyer. Do your banking at a bank."

Fees are a constant source of temptation for many lawyers. It is the one aspect of practicing law in which the lawyer and client are in potential conflict. The client wants to pay less, while the lawyer wants to charge more. I sometimes envy the British barristers of old, who never had to deal with clients directly over fees — or anything else. They were hired by the solicitors who paid them. I have in my office an old barrister's fee box from the nineteenth century, into which the solicitor would discreetly deposit the fee. I keep it to remind me of the days when law was a "learned profession," rather than a business.

Today law is very much a business, with the large law firms behaving indistinguishably from other giant corporations focused on the bottom line. If you become a private lawyer, you are necessarily becoming a businessman or woman, but the bottom line need not be measured by money alone.

20
Stop Whining, Start Winning

Whenever I feel down about anything, I eavesdrop on the chat room of greedyassociates.com. Listening to five minutes of mega-whining from a bunch of rich, spoiled brats makes me feel a lot better about my problems. First, a gripe from "Francine":

> *$165,000 is just not as much as you think.*
>
> *Take out $70,000 for taxes. That's 95,000.*
>
> *Then there's a broker's fee (2500), rent (1200 a month), food (200 a month) clothes ($2000 a year, say). That comes to 30,000 a year. You're left with $40,000.*
>
> *Now say you have loans that you took out from [sic] for undergrad and law school totaling $90,000.*
>
> *Say you pay $25,000 a year for it. That leaves you with $15,000!*

Now a whine from "illegaleagle" trying to prove "that we're not completely spoiled":

> *$125,000 plus a supposed 35,000 bonus = 160,000 minus fed taxes at 30% (48,000) = 112,000 minus social security tax (approx 4,400) = 170,000 minus state and city tax (approx 14,000) = 93,000 minus law school loans (say 1800/mo) = 71,400 minus the extra 1,200/mo that an apartment costs in NYC versus almost any other place in the whole damn world = 57,000.*
>
> *So all of a sudden . . . you're in Al Gore's middle class, not George Bush's top 1%.*

Finally a challenge from "Ivan the Terrible":

> *I'd like to hear from at least one "genuinely" happy corporate attorney out there — and please don't give me that bull shit that you feed those 2L summer interns. I am not impressed by horseshit like "uh, I've worked (made photocopies) on several billion dollar deals — woopie [sic]."*
>
> *Let's be honest people — our profession sucks the big one.*

These young men and women are making more money in a year — in both absolute and relative terms — than most people around the world earn in their lifetime. And there's not a lot of heavy lifting required. Sure, the hours are long and the partners demanding, but what do they expect for these salaries? If they can't take that kind of pressure in their twenties, how are they going to deal with the increasing responsibilities of partnership? This is, after all, a period of testing and learning. So no one should expect to be coddled.

The whining doesn't really surprise me, since it often begins in law school. Many students, who beat out heavy competition to make it to places like Harvard, demand an end to competition and grading as soon as they arrive. They don't like the Socratic method because it puts them on the spot. They demand speech codes to protect them from "offensive" comments. They want to be paid like adults, but treated like children when it comes to the rough-and-tumble of the real world.

Well, sorry, but if you can't take the heat, pick a different profession — one that pays less. If you want to be among the most highly paid professionals in the world, work for it and stop griping. If Harvard is too competitive for you, pick a less competitive law school. If the hours at Cravath are too long, go to a firm that pays half as much and gives you more time off. Nobody is forcing anyone to aspire to the top rungs of the highest paid profession, but if you do, you have no right to bring down the standards.

There are plenty of options out there. Do public interest work. Defend capital cases. Work on environmental cases. These jobs, too, require hard work, but they may be more gratifying. They certainly don't pay as well, but high pay comes with a price tag — hard work and long hours. You are in control of your own destiny. Stop griping and start choosing. You can always open up your own firm, either alone or with a friend or two. It won't be easy, but at least you can decide how hard you want to work. If you pursue this path, it's important to leave the big firm on positive terms, so they will be inclined to refer cases to you, if they're too small for them or if they have a conflict. The drawback of having your own firm is that you will have nobody to whine about, but if you get really successful, maybe you'll be able to hire some associates who can whine about you.

Young associates used to have the excuse that they were victims of a bait and switch. There was an old joke about the devil offering a third-year law student a free look at Hell. The associate sees beautiful, happy people, eating well and having fun, and so he becomes a sinner. When he finally dies and goes to Hell permanently, it's a very different place with fire and misery. He complains to the Devil, reminding him of what he had previously been shown. The Devil replies, "That was our summer associates program." But today — thanks to greedyassociates.com and other information sources — no one has the right to claim surprise. You know full well what awaits you at the big firms, and you have chosen that path. So stop complaining. Either do your job or change it. There's nothing attractive about a whining rich kid.

Part TWO

Winning and Losing

21
Where Can You Learn Advocacy?

One bit of advice that I will repeat in different contexts throughout this book is that a lawyer's education is far too important to be left entirely to law schools. No school, regardless of how good it may be, is capable of teaching the potential lawyer all there is to know about the profession (and business) of law. Having said that, it is important to add that a lawyer's education is also too important to be left entirely to practicing lawyers. An excellent legal education requires a balance of classroom, courtroom and office experience. This is especially true of the education of trial lawyers.

For generations, many of our best law schools have failed in their mission to educate first-rate trial lawyers. Indeed, it is fair to say that most first-rate trial lawyers did not attend first-rate law schools. The law school at which I teach — Harvard — bears some of the responsibility. Back in the nineteenth century, its dean, Christopher Columbus Langdell, developed the appellate-case method of teaching substantive law, legal doctrine, legal theory and procedure. Emphasis is placed on appellate decision — that is, opinions rendered by courts of appeals, primarily on issues of law. That is understandable, since American law is largely judge-made, and our appeals courts are the primary makers of law. (Legislatures, of course, enact statutes, but statutes generally are very broad in application and rarely resolve specific disputes.)

What American law schools often do not teach — at least do not teach well enough — are the basis skills of advocacy: how to prepare a case, how to examine a witness, how to argue before a jury, how to write a brief and how to argue before appellate judges. One of the understandable reasons why law professors don't emphasize these skills is that many of them simply do not have experience or expertise in them. Law professors are selected, at least at many schools, not because of their skills as practicing lawyers, but because of their reputations as legal scholars and teachers. In fact, many law professors would probably make excellent advocates, since classroom teaching bears some striking resemblances to courtroom advocacy; law teaching is not one of those professions where "those who can, do, while those who can't, teach."

For whatever reasons, it remains true that an honors graduate of an elite law school can enter upon the practice of law without the slightest inkling of what it takes to be a successful advocate. For the most part, students have been told to go out into the world and observe those who are thought to possess these skills. The problem is that most students don't have the foggiest notion of how to recognize a skilled advocate when they see one. Advocacy is not a skill that is always apparent, especially in the brief observations that most students are able to make of practicing lawyers. Accordingly, students occasionally confuse articulateness with advocacy. Though articulateness may be a prerequisite to effective advocacy, it is not a substitute for it. Students, and indeed clients, often confuse smooth sartorial splendor, good looks and charm with effective advocacy. Again, these fortunate attributes may certainly help a lawyer persuade a jury (or even a judge). But, in my experience, some of the worst advocates I have ever seen have been smooth, charming, good-looking — and stupid. And some of the best have been unkempt, forgetful (of personal details) and rough around the edges. I recall a *New Yorker* cartoon depicting two clients in a lawyer's waiting room discussing their lawyer, who can be seen at his desk dressed in a clown suit. "He must be good," one of them says, "if he can get away with dressing like that."

I also remember watching an appellate argument during the first days of my clerkship and being blown away by the skills of one particular Justice Department lawyer. He anticipated the judge's questions, using his answers not only to respond to the judge's concerns, but also to advance his arguments. He was a master of the facts and the law. At lunch a few hours later, several of the clerks were discussing the argument. One began by opining that the lawyer wasn't very good. Surprised, I asked him why. "Did you notice his shoes?" he asked rhetorically. "They were brown and unpolished." No, I hadn't noticed, and neither had the judges. Nor did they seem concerned about his rumpled suit. I later asked Judge Bazelon what he thought of the lawyer, and he assured me that he was one of the best around.

Law students also frequently confuse intelligence with effective advocacy. Again, a high degree of intelligence is certainly important for effective advocacy, but it is by no means a substitute. I have heard some of the smartest people I know make some of the least effective arguments before judges and juries. Effective advocacy is one of the most difficult attributes to identify in a potential or practicing lawyer. It may take years to develop and hone that skill — really a collection of skills — into the finished product of which the advocate is justly proud.

Sure, there are hints, shortcuts, blind alleys to be avoided, and other handy tools of the trade to be picked up — and in the forthcoming essays I will mention some of those — but the key is hard work.

In real life, cases are rarely won in the courtroom. Dazzling cross-examination almost never produces "Perry Mason moments." In civil cases there is little courtroom drama, because the witnesses have been deposed in advance of the trial. Indeed, the mantra of the civil trial is "no surprises." And most turn out to be like opening night of a Broadway show that has been rehearsed endlessly before its premiere. Criminal trials do occasionally generate some excitement, but almost never of the sort that is the staple of Hollywood movies or TV courtroom dramas. Cases are won and lost in preparation — in the library and in the field.

Too many lawyers depend on their "courtroom skills" and downplay the preparation necessary to take advantage of their skills. As an appellate lawyer, I have probably read as many transcripts of losing criminal trials as anyone, and if there is one common theme, it is lack of preparation. Lawyers with great reputations come into the courtroom strutting their stuff but unfamiliar with governing case law, modern DNA technology and the background of critical witnesses.

No law school graduate should regard his or her legal education as complete unless he or she has begun to develop skills of advocacy. Every lawyer, at bottom, is an advocate. Law is an adversarial profession. And the skills necessary to make a good trial lawyer are also helpful in making an effective office advocate, negotiation advocate or consumer advocate. So take advocacy courses if they are offered by experienced and excellent lawyers, go to court and watch trials and — most important — try to spend some time working for the best advocate who will hire you. Then combine all this together and go out and begin to learn for yourself.

22 Winning Before a Jury: The "Aha" Theory

Although I have participated in far fewer trials in front of juries than in appellate and other legal arguments in front of judges, I have done enough consulting in, and reading the transcripts of, jury trials to offer some guidance. In addition to the usual advice — prepare thoroughly, cross-examine sparingly and modulate your advocacy — I offer some iconoclastic suggestions.

The first is generally to reject advice that begins with the word "never" or "always." Some older lawyers advise rookies "never" to put their clients on the witness stand in a criminal case. I believe the decision whether to waive the right to testify in one's own behalf is about the most difficult tactical decision a client must make during a trial. Since most criminal defendants are convicted by juries, whatever decision is made about testifying will be blamed for the loss. I generally meet defendants shortly after they are convicted, and one of the first things they say is that their [expletive deleted] trial lawyer really screwed up by "putting me on the stand" or by "not putting me on the stand." It's a no-win situation for the trial lawyer, even if the clients themselves made the ultimate decision — as they are supposed to do, at least in theory. The trial lawyer always gets the blame, but rarely the credit. (When a lawyer wins a case on behalf of a client, the client generally doesn't want to have anything to do with the lawyer, because he doesn't want to be reminded of the trial and because he convinces himself that it was his own innocence, and not the advocacy of the lawyer, that won the case.)

The decision whether to have a defendant testify is so difficult because it really does matter in most cases. Juries want to hear from a defendant who is claiming to be innocent. "If he has nothing to hide, why is he hiding behind the Fifth Amendment?" That's what many jurors ask themselves, despite the judge's instruction to them not to draw any incriminating inferences from a defendant's invocation of the constitutional right not to testify.

So why not put your client on the witness stand? There are several very good reasons. First, he's probably guilty, regardless of what he told you. As a statistical matter, a large majority of defendants who stand trial before juries are factually guilty. If you know for sure that your client is guilty — if he confessed to you or gave you evidence that leaves no doubt of his guilt — then you may not allow him to testify and commit perjury in answer to your questions. Criminal defendants know this rule, and very few ever confess their guilt to their lawyers. I have had only one such confession in the hundreds of cases on which I have worked, and in that case my client had already confessed to a policeman before I became his lawyer. (We won the case on constitutional grounds unrelated to guilt or innocence.)

In most cases the lawyer is free to advise the client either to take the stand or not. In many cases, the decision is a no-brainer, because the defendant will not only make a terrible witness, but his testimony will also open the door to prosecution evidence that would be inadmissible if the defendant remains silent. Such evidence might include prior crimes committed by the defendant, negative testimony about his reputation and character, as well as rebuttal witnesses. Sometimes, it's a no-brainer even if your client would make a good witness and not open the door to adverse testimony. For example, in cases in which the defense has focused on the misconduct or negligence of the police, the incompetence of the forensic labs or the weakness of the government's experts, it might be a mistake to shift the focus back to the defendant. Once a defendant testifies, the jury tends to minimize the testimony of other witnesses and to focus on whether they believe the defendant. That is why, in the O.J. Simpson case, it was a no-brainer to advise against his taking the stand. In the absence of his testimony, the jury focused on the police, the forensic experts and the ineptness of the prosecutors in, for example, having Simpson try on the gloves in front of the jury. This played to our strength. But these prosecutorial blunders would all have become insignificant if Simpson had taken center stage and testified, as they did when he testified at the civil trial and lost.

Most criminal defendants think they will make good witnesses, since many of them have been conning people all their lives. They generally want to testify, and have to be talked out of it by their lawyers. Most criminal defense lawyers prefer not to have their clients testify, and for good reason. Sometimes, the lawyer simply makes the decision on a knee-jerk basis, invoking the "n" word: "I never put my clients on." But there are some situations in which a defendant should testify, and it is the job of a good lawyer to evaluate all the considerations and give the right advice for each particular client. For example, in insanity defense cases, it is often a good idea to have the defendant testify, if his testimony will demonstrate his insanity. In such a case, the defendant is really being used as an exhibit rather than as a witness. Lawyers should make "retail" decisions on a case-by-case basis, rather than "wholesale" decisions based on general presuppositions.

Another "never" rule that is taught to most young lawyers is "Never ask a question to which you don't know the answer." That is certainly true of direct examination of friendly witnesses in both civil and criminal cases. If you have prepared your witnesses well, there should be no surprises on direct. But the "never" rule is also applied to cross-examination, and it has validity in civil cases where adverse witnesses have generally been deposed and interrogated prior to the trial. But in criminal cases, it should not be a "never" rule. Of course, it is far better to know the answer to every cross-examination question before you ask it, and it is sometimes possible to ask closed-ended questions to which the witness has locked in favorable answers by previous statements or actions. Other times it may be possible to checkmate the witness by asking a question with two possible answers — each of which can be turned to the advantage of your client. If he answers A, that answer corroborated your case, and if he answers B, you can prove that he is lying. In such cases, you need not know in advance which answer he will give, since either one will help your client. But on occasion, a good defense attorney must take calculated risks based on an assessment of probabilities. When the case against your client is very strong and it appears as if you are almost certainly going to lose, it may well be to the client's advantage for you to ask some risky questions — so long as the potential benefits are commensurate with the risks.

There is a wonderful song in the Gilbert and Sullivan operetta *Pinafore*, in which the captain is singing his own praises, while the crew serves as the chorus. Every time the captain proclaims an absolute virtue, such as never getting sick at sea or using foul language, the crew challenges him:

"What, never?"

And he responds, "No, never."

The crew persists in the challenge "What, never?" and the captain finally has to acknowledge, "Well, hardly ever."

So when you are told "never" to employ a particular tactic (if it's permissible and ethical), think "hardly ever."

Regarding the more general aspects of jury advocacy, I have one piece of advice that may sound counterintuitive, but which I am convinced is correct. Try not to let the jury believe that you are trying to talk them into anything.

Let *them* come to the conclusion you want them to reach. I call this the "Aha" theory of advocacy. In my novel *Just Revenge*, I explain the origin of the term "Aha":

> *Aha had become a code word in the Ringel family for the style Abe had developed over the years of asking the rhetorical questions during his argument. It got the jurors to interact with him. He strongly believed that the most effective advocacy occurred not when the lawyer shoved an argument down the throat of a juror, but rather when the lawyer allowed the juror to come up with the argument or at least think he had. It gave the juror a greater stake in the argument. Abe called this the "aha theory of advocacy" after the joke Haskell had once told him about the Jewish man who had ordered chicken soup in the same restaurant every night for years. This time the waiter noticed the customer wasn't eating it, so he asked him, "Is it too*

> *hot?" No answer. "Too cold?" No answer. "Is there a fly in it?" No answer. Finally, in frustration, the waiter said, "I'm gonna taste it myself and see what's wrong." The waiter came over to taste it, but there is no spoon. The customer looks at the waiter and says, "Aha!"*
>
> *Abe believed that jurors were like the waiter. They had to discover for themselves what was missing, and then you could say, "Aha!"*

A lawyer should never be perceived as a salesman trying to sell the jury a bill of goods. Jurors resent being talked into anything. They may nod in apparent agreement while you are making your pitch, but when they go back to the jury room without you, they will want to think for themselves. Remember *Twelve Angry Men!*

23 Winning Before a Judge: Political Justice

If winning is all you care about, there is one simple rule: Pick your cases carefully. If having a good won-and-lost record is your only goal, you can achieve a near-perfect record by litigating only sure winners. Cases to be decided by a judge, as distinguished from a jury, can be divided into two major categories. The first consists of those cases in which the judge has no stake, except doing justice. Theoretically, all cases should fall into this category, since judges take an oath to administer justice "without respect to person. . . ." But in the real world, many judges have a significant stake in the outcome of a great many cases. The stake may be career-based: He or she aspires to reelection or promotion to a higher court, and that goal would be made more difficult by ruling in favor of or against a particular litigant. This phenomenon is particularly influential in criminal cases. Judges who are perceived, whether accurately or not, as "soft on crime" are less likely to be reelected or promoted. Recall the case of federal judge Harold Baer in New York who properly ruled that drugs found in the trunk of a car had to be suppressed because they were seized in violation of the Constitution. All hell broke loose. It was during the 1996 presidential campaign and he was condemned by both candidates. His prospects for promotion were forever ruined, even though he succumbed to the pressure and subsequently reversed his ruling. The message delivered by the presidential candidates was unmistakably clear: If you want to be promoted, side against criminals, even if the Constitution requires you to rule in their favor.

Another story carries the same lesson for judges. When John Ashcroft was being considered for attorney general, there was controversy over the role he had played in preventing the promotion of an African-American state court judge to the federal bench. He was accused of racial bias. His response was that he was biased against the judge not because he was black, but because he had voted to reverse several capital cases. *That* kind of bias was deemed entirely acceptable and Ashcroft was confirmed. Again, the message to judges regarding criminal defendants is clear: When in doubt, don't let them out.

So don't expect a fair shake in criminal cases. You won't get it. The heavy thumb of careerism is on the scale of justice in nearly every criminal case, certainly in high-profile cases involving unpopular defendants. It's gotten so bad that I prefer to argue appeals in front of conservative octogenarian judges than moderate young judges, since the former have no further ambitions and my client had some chance at getting an objective assessment of his legal claims.

Criminal cases, though the most extreme, are not the only ones in which some judges have a stake. Judges are political beings, since most judgeships grow out of loyalty to a party or a politician. As the old saw goes: A state judge is a lawyer who knew a governor, and a federal judge is a lawyer who knew a senator. This is not always the case, and some judges are appointed because of other factors — race, religion, ethnicity, gender, political ideology and, on occasion, even brilliance. I am not aware of a single judge who was appointed — at least in recent times — on the basis of "judicial philosophy," despite the claim that this is always the major factor. Most governors, senators, presidents and voters have no idea what a judicial — as distinguished from a political — philosophy actually is, since it deals with esoteric issues such as judicial restraint, federalism, the role of precedent and the appropriate tools to be employed in interpreting the law.[1]

If most judges are appointed primarily because they are expected to reach particular results in certain kinds of cases — criminal, abortion, religious, racial — many of them will reach these results whenever possible. Some will disappoint their appointers, while others will decide only close cases in accordance with their "mandate."

It is important for lawyers to understand the personal dynamics that drive ambitious judges in these sorts of cases. It would be naïve in the extreme to ignore the very real impact these extrinsic factors have on judicial decisions, and lawyers are paid for their experience, not their naiveté. Different lawyers will deal with these realities in very different ways. Few will confront the issue directly, because to do so would be to accuse the judges of violating their judicial oath.

One reason I do not enjoy arguing cases to the Supreme Court is that by the time you get up to argue, the justices have generally made up their minds. When they decide to take a case — and they take very few — they ordinarily know how it is going to come out. Nothing a lawyer says or writes can change their minds, especially on big ideological issues, such as abortion, capital punishment, religion and race. Justice Thomas may have sworn under oath that he had never discussed the constitutionality of abortion, implying that he had an open mind on the issue, but I don't know many people who believed him. When the first major abortion case came before him, he left little doubt that his mind had always been closed. As Jeffrey Toobin observed in "The Burden of Clarence Thomas" (*New Yorker*, Sept. 27, 1993, p. 47):

> *Since it was the most famous Supreme Court case of his generation, this statement drew widespread skepticism at the time. In any event, it appears that*

> *Thomas had made up his mind about the fate of Roe before he arrived on the Court; without even discussing the issue with his law clerks, he decided that the case should be overturned. "There was no point in talking about Casey," the source says. "There was no doubt whatsoever on where he was coming out. There was no discussion at all." Thomas joined Justice Scalia's dissenting opinion, which urged that Roe be overturned.*
>
> *This has led Professor Pamela Karlan to conclude: "I think he perjured himself about Roe" (Savage, "In the Matter of Justice,"* Los Angeles Times, *Oct. 9, 1994).*

Even in death penalty cases, a majority of the justices have sent a powerful message that no briefs or arguments will ever change their minds. In two cases in which certiorari was granted — only four votes are needed to allow full argument and briefing — the five justices who opposed certiorari voted against staying the execution.[2] Even when human life is at stake, these justices will not come to court with a sufficiently open mind that allows for the possibility that even one of them might be persuaded by the briefs or arguments of counsel. There is no professional or personal gratification in arguing to a bunch of closed-minded automatons. As one lawyer put it, "It's like arguing with a vending machine that took your money and didn't give you the Coca Cola."

In civil cases in which the judge has no possible stake or interest in the outcome beyond seeing that justice is done, the skill of the lawyer can really make a difference. The facts and the law will still matter more, but it is possible for a great lawyer to win a losing case and for a poor lawyer to lose a winning case. One of the keys to being a successful advocate is to understand the differences among types of cases from the outset and to plan your strategy accordingly.

24

Arguing in the Supreme Court

A double capital case I argued before the United States Supreme Court several years ago may help to illustrate the problem of arguing to judges who have already made up their minds. It persuaded me — perhaps more than any other single experience in my career as a lawyer — how unfairly the death penalty is administered.

My clients were two young men. They were eighteen and nineteen years old when they "broke" their father out of prison. The boys believed that their father was a good man in prison on a bum rap. The entire plan had been designed to ensure that no one would get hurt. And no one was hurt during the breakout itself.

But then their getaway car had a flat and the father ordered his sons to wave down another car. The car that stopped contained an entire family: father, mother, baby, niece and even a dog. After exchanging cars at gunpoint, the father sent the boys away to get water for the family. But it was a trick. When the boys left to get them water, their father murdered the whole family.

The father escaped, but was soon found dead in the Arizona desert. Eventually, the boys were caught and convicted of murdering the family, even though they never fired a shot and never intended that anyone be killed. Since they had conspired with their father to break him out of jail, they were held responsible for his crimes. The boys were sentenced to death.

I got to know the boys during the many years I worked on their appeal. They are good boys. They were never in trouble before or since. They didn't hurt anyone. They were shocked and devastated by their father's brutal murders, but they could do nothing to stop him.

The case was an interesting one, with complex and subtle legal issues. When I argued it, the justices were obviously intrigued by the issues, but most of them seemed to have made up their minds.

I had spent long hours trying to anticipate every one of the justices' questions and prepared appropriate answers. But what if I missed a few? What if I made an "error"? What if I didn't think quickly enough on my feet? Should my failings as an attorney be a cause of the execution of two young men?

The obvious answer is that lawyers don't *cause* executions — the criminals themselves cause their sentences by the crimes they have committed. But this is too simple a response that conveys only a half-truth. It fails to account for the reality that far fewer than 1 percent of all persons whose crimes make them eligible for execution have, in fact, been put to death over the past two decades. The prisons of our nation — the "life" rows — are populated with thousands of real murderers who deliberately killed and did not receive the death penalty.

The two boys whose lives I argued for were not on death row because of their crimes alone, but rather because of factors extraneous to their crimes. First, they refused to accept a plea bargain that would have required them to testify against their mother; second, the publicity given to their father's crimes; and finally, the fact that the sentence was imposed by a particularly harsh judge in a state with a particularly harsh capital punishment statute. In other cases, the determining factors are the race of the victims and the defendants (in this case, both were white) and the quality of legal representation at the trial.

Before I argued the case, I knew — as an intellectual matter — that many random factors could mean the difference between life and death in a capital case. But actually being up in front of the justices trying to answer their questions brought it home to me with the emotional impact of a jolt of electricity. One justice (Scalia) asked me whether it would be constitutional to execute an armed robber who "threw his gun" to his accomplice, who then shot and killed a pursuing policeman. It was a clever question that I would have been delighted to debate for hours in an academic setting. But this wasn't an academic question, and a great deal might have been riding on my answer. If I answered no, I might discredit the remainder of my argument, and if I answered yes, I might concede a principle that the justice could then expand to apply to my case.

I tried to duck the question by pointing out that my clients' case was different, since they intended to keep the family alive by getting them water, whereas the armed robber intended to help his accomplice shoot at the police. But the justice insisted that I answer his question directly. I still wonder whether the answer I gave — that execution would be impermissible in the tossed-gun hypothesis — helped or hurt my clients. (I doubt it made any difference.) One thing I do know, however, is that a system of deciding life-and-death issues on the basis of the cleverness of a lawyer's answer to hypothetical questions is not a just system.

Regardless of whether one favors or opposes the death penalty, I believe that all reasonable people must be appalled at the indisputable fact that whether a convicted murderer lives or dies may turn not so much on his personal culpability as on his lawyer's skills, the victim's race, the defendant's willingness to plea bargain, the judge's predisposition in favor of the death penalty and other extraneous factors.

The Supreme Court eventually ruled against my clients by a vote of 5—4, but the justices remanded the case to the Arizona courts, where we eventually persuaded the state judges to vacate their death sentences. Good lawyering, in my experience, often makes more of a difference in the lower courts than in the Supreme Court.

25

Who Is Your Client?

The Bible warns against serving two masters. So do the rules of professional ethics. Though your client is not your master, you must indeed serve only him or her whenever you act in a representational capacity. When you are a lawyer working for a client, you are neither liberal nor conservative, black nor white, man nor woman, Jew nor Christian. You are whatever is in the legitimate best interest of your client.

I confronted a conflict between my long-held ideology and my professional obligations in the capital case described in the prior chapter. After we lost the initial appeals in the Arizona Supreme Court, we decided to apply for review in the U.S. Supreme Court. All the experts warned us that we were going to lose. They had counted noses and realized that a recent change of personnel in the Court had made it clear that the conservative justices were looking for a case like this one in which to reverse or limit a prior ruling that had prohibited the infliction of the death penalty on a nontriggerman — that is, a conspirator who himself had not killed the victim or intended his death. I, too, could count noses and realized that we had a long shot, at best, of winning. But I also knew that we had some chance of losing in the Supreme Court with a decision that opened up various possibilities for further litigation in the Arizona courts.

I was thus confronted with an exquisitely delicate conflict between what was best for the dozens of nontriggermen who, under then-existing law, could not be executed, and my own clients, who had been sentenced to death and, without some judicial intervention, would surely be executed. There was considerable pressure from institutional opponents of the death penalty not to bring this case to the court. I could not, however, succumb to that pressure. While representing my two clients, I was required to wear the kind of blinders that are put on horses to make sure they look straight ahead and not to either side. I could not properly look to the interest of *other* death-row inmates or to the broad campaign against the death penalty of which I was a part. It was painful for me to make a tactical legal decision for my clients that I knew would hurt my cause, but I had no choice. The lives of these two young men were in my hands and my hands alone. I was their advocate. There were many others out there who were advocates for the anti–death penalty cause and for the other death-row inmates. But Ricky and Raymond Tyson had only me (and my associates).

It turned out exactly as we had all anticipated. The Supreme Court used our case to reverse an earlier precedent that had limited the death penalty. Several other inmates who might well have been spared execution were executed. But Ricky and Raymond Tyson were saved. A majority of the Supreme Court remanded their case to the Arizona courts for further findings, and we were able to use the remand to reverse their death penalties. I did not celebrate even when we learned that Ricky and Raymond Tyson would not be executed, because I knew that others would be, in part because of the decision we had taken in Ricky and Raymond Tyson's case.

These are the kinds of tough, zero-sum decisions that often have to be made when a lawyer's professional obligation to his client clashes with that lawyer's ideological commitment to a cause.

26 Losing

So you just lost your first big case. You're devastated. You worked so hard. Your client was counting on you, you argued well, but the court has ruled against you. The first question you have to ask yourself is: Did you lose, or was it your client who lost? I do not mean this question in the cynical way in which famed lawyer Edward Bennett Williams once allegedly responded to a losing client after he had lost a case. The client asked, "Where do we go from here?" Williams replied: "What do you mean 'we'? I go back to my comfortable office, and you go to jail." I mean to ask the question in a somewhat different way. Sometimes lawyers lose winning cases for their client. But most good lawyers who lose cases never had a chance. The facts are against them, the law was against them. Their client deserved to lose. Oh, sure, occasionally a lawyer can snatch victory from the jaws of defeat and win a losing case. Just as often, a lawyer can snatch defeat from the jaws of victory and lose a winning case, but most lawyers win the winners and lose the losers. That's why if your only goal as a lawyer is to win, it's not so hard to do; just pick winning cases. But it's not the goal only to win. It would be as if a doctor wanted only perfect outcomes and never wanted to lose a patient. It would be pretty easy to become a podiatrist or a cosmetic surgeon. Doctors who fix feet and straighten out noses rarely end up with fatalities. It's the brain surgeons and the heart surgeons who lose patients. But it's the same brain and heart surgeons who save lives. The same is true for lawyers. Those who take the most difficult cases lose most often. But they also can occasionally win extremely difficult cases. That's the thrill of advocacy.

27
Don't Underestimate Your Opponent

I had a friend who put herself through law school playing poker. She was an attractive woman from rural Alabama with long blond hair and a working-class southern accent. Her modus operandi was to lull her opponents into seeing her as a stereotype — a dumb, southern, blond woman, certainly inexperienced at poker. Her opponents underestimated her, and that provided her with the competitive edge necessary to win.

Remember that story when you evaluate your opponents in a case. Never underestimate them. Always assume they're at least as smart as you are. Try to think like them. Get into their heads, their hearts and their skin. If they're any good, they're doing the same thing in regard to you.

Remember, they think they're on the right side of the case, just as you do. The ability of lawyers to rationalize their positions is unlimited. Defense lawyers often develop what I call DLBS — defense lawyers' blind spot. They refuse to see the evidence of their client's guilt, even when it is staring them in the eye. They need to believe their clients are innocent in order to defend them zealously. Prosecutors develop a different kind of blind spot, as I explain in the next chapter.

Give your opposing lawyer the benefit of the doubt in evaluating his or her intelligence, motivation and sense of justice. It's always better to be overprepared than underprepared.

28
The Prosecutor's Blind Spot

Prosecutors are today's heroes. These lawyers in white hats often go on to higher elected office. In the minds of many citizens, they can do no wrong — so long as they put the bad guys behind bars. But there is a darker side of prosecution. Many decent and honest prosecutors are willing to do almost anything to convict people they believe to be guilty — and they are praised for it.

In an age of decreasing judicial supervision over our criminal justice system, it is more important than ever to hold prosecutors to exacting standards of fairness, legality and ethics. Despite the theoretically adversarial nature of our system, the prosecutor is among the most important arbiters of justice. The virtually unreviewable discretion of prosecutorial decisions — investigating, immunizing, plea-bargaining, allocating resources and others — gives the prosecutor quasijudicial responsibilities.

Prosecutorial misconduct, however, is rampant. Even if one looks only at the reported cases, the quantity and variety of alleged misconduct are staggering. The reported cases constitute only a very small percentage of the actual instances of misconduct, since many defense lawyers are apt to shut their eyes to the misdeeds of their brothers and sisters at the bar. "What do you want to get another lawyer in trouble for?" I have heard that refrain so many times that the sentence completes itself after the first few words. Lawyers — even the most vigorous defense attorneys — are often inclined to place the interests of occupational camaraderie over the interests of their clients. Many lawyers rationalize their silence in the face of outrageous prosecutorial misconduct by arguing that it is in their future clients' interest to stay on the "good side of the prosecutor." While this may be true, the real reason for not blowing the whistle may have more to do with the future interest of the lawyer than with his clients. Moreover, when a lawyer is representing a particular client, that is whose legitimate interests he is supposed to be serving, not some hypothetical future client he hopes to get.

The problem is likely to get worse. As the Supreme Court begins to turn its traffic light from red to yellow and even green, prosecutors will be deterred less often — some might say encouraged — to adopt an "end-justifies-the-means" approach. They too will apply their individual cost-benefit constitutional analyses that have come to characterize recent Supreme Court opinions in the exclusionary rule area. If the Supreme Court nearly always finds that the cost of strictly complying with the Bill of

Rights outweighs its benefits, it is not difficult to conjecture how most prosecutors will arrive at their sums in this constitutional calculus.

The role of the vigorous defense attorney — prepared to do battle against prosecutorial misconduct — is becoming increasingly important in the overall struggle to maintain our Bill of Rights. In order for defense counsel to perform this function, they must come to believe that it is not only in the interest of the Constitution to combat prosecutorial misconduct, but that it can also be in the interest of the client. Defense attorneys must be given the tools to convert prosecutorial misconduct into favorable results for their clients.

An important tool in combating wrongdoing is a clear understanding of the motives, causes and reasons underlying the evil. Yet very little has been written about *why* prosecutors engage in misconduct. Most prosecutors — even those who misbehave egregiously — are decent human beings. Many of my own students go on to become prosecutors. They do not think they are hatching diabolical plots to convict the innocent. They believe they are doing their job fairly.

There are, of course, rare exceptions. Occasionally one hears about a truly dishonest prosecutor who is willing to convict the innocent to enhance his reputation or serve some other political interest.

But I am convinced that the vast majority of prosecutors who engage in the typical sort of misconduct — allowing police witnesses to lie, failing to turn over evidence favorable to the defendant, pandering to the fears of jurors — do so out of what they regard as the noblest of motives: the need to convict the guilty and reduce the scourge of crime. They can justify this "ends-justifies-the-means" attitude by pointing to the Supreme Court's cost-benefit approach to the exclusionary rule and the harmless error doctrine.

The vast majority of prosecutorial misconduct occurs in cases involving guilty defendants. That is so for an obvious reason: The vast majority of criminal cases involve guilty defendants. If I am correct in observing that most prosecutorial misconduct is directed against guilty defendants, then it follows that most prosecutors do not view their misconduct as hindering the "search for truth." Instead they see their actions as calculated to produce a true verdict: the conviction of a guilty defendant. It is the defense attorney — the person who is seeking to get his guilty client acquitted — who is hindering the search for truth.

There are, of course, many layers of "truth" in a criminal case. The ultimate truth is the guilt or innocence — generally the guilt — of the defendant. Another "truth" is the credibility of the prosecutor's substantive witness. Even that "truth" is often subdivided into parts. The first issue is whether the witness is telling the rough truth about whether the defendant did what he is accused of doing. Prosecutors almost always try to ensure that this first level of witness-truth is told. The second level of witness-truth, however, is often neglected. It is whether the government's witness is telling the whole truth about his own background and general credibility.

Prosecutors who believe that their witness is telling the truth about the defendant's guilt often worry that if the whole truth about the witness's background emerges, the jury will be conned by a clever defense attorney into disbelieving the true testimony about the crime. Of course, defense attorneys who know that the government's witness is telling the truth about their guilty client's commission of the crime try to persuade the jury to disbelieve that testimony because the witness is a "sleaze."

Every experienced lawyer has participated in a variation on the following dialogue:

> DEFENSE ATTORNEY "Ladies and gentleman of the jury. You've heard the government's main witness admit that he is a con man, a crook and a liar. How can you believe anything he testified to in this courtroom?"
>
> PROSECUTING ATTORNEY (who gets the last word) "Of course my witness isn't the kind of man any of us would like to have to dinner. But I didn't pick him as *my* associate. The defendant did. And when you are prosecuting the devil, you don't go to heaven for witnesses; you have to go to hell. But just because the witness has a bad background doesn't mean he isn't telling the truth this time."

Juries generally accept the prosecutor's argument. But sometimes the government must, of necessity, rely upon a witness with such an egregious background that there is a risk that the jurors will disbelieve him — if they learn the full extent of his crimes and lies. In that case, even a well-intentioned prosecutor may be tempted to fudge or hide the facts about his witness's nefarious background.

There may be other reasons, as well, why a prosecutor may consciously or unconsciously allow his witness to withhold the whole truth about his background.

Let me describe a case that I litigated near the beginning of my career. (The case became the basis for the best-selling book and movie *Prince of the City* and is described from a different vantage point in my book *The Best Defense*.) The defendant was a criminal lawyer, despised by many U.S. attorneys, who believed that he made a practice of creating false alibis. He was indicted for agreeing to pay an undercover cop for secret information. The main evidence against him was the testimony of the cop and some tapes. The cop testified at trial about the transactions. He was then asked about his own background and admitted to having committed three crimes while he was in the drug unit. The truth, as it later emerged, was quite different. He had committed literally hundreds of crimes, including perjury, heroin dealing, destruction of evidence and bribery. It is clear, in retrospect, that some of the prosecutors must have suspected that he was withholding the full story of his criminal background. (The policeman later confirmed that to me.) Yet these highly respected prosecutors failed to press him or to conduct an independent investigation. They closed their eyes and allowed him to lie — not about the guilt or innocence of the defendant, but about his own background.

There were, in my opinion, two reasons for this kind of prosecutorial misconduct. The first, and most conventional, is the fear that if the jury learned that the principal witness was a major criminal, they would simply refuse to convict the defendant. As one juror told me, "If I had known the truth about [the policeman's] criminal past and known that he had committed numerous crimes and had lied I would not have believed [his] testimony and I would not have voted for conviction."[1]

The second reason is that the prosecutors were afraid that their witness would simply refuse to testify if he had to admit publicly that he — and his police colleagues — were so corrupt.

In the end, the misconduct was rewarded. The defendant was convicted; his conviction was affirmed through many appeals, on the grounds that if there was any misconduct, it constituted harmless error; the lying policeman was never prosecuted for perjury; and the prosecutors who allowed him to testify falsely were promoted and praised for their actions.

The message sent to young prosecutors by disgraceful episodes like this one — episodes that occur all over the country — is threefold: (1) If misconduct is necessary to convict a guilty defendant, by all means do it; (2) try not to get caught, because that may complicate matters; (3) but if you do get caught, you can count on the court to bail you out, either by ignoring the misconduct or by invoking the "harmless error" rule.

What, after all, *is* the harmless error rule? It is basically a judicial assurance that nearly anything will be tolerated in regard to an obviously guilty defendant. If the defendant is so obviously guilty, then basically any misconduct by a prosecutor will not have made the difference between conviction and acquittal.

What lessons about "the search for truth" can be drawn from this account? Some very mixed ones. Prosecutors will argue that truth prevailed, and they may be right. A defendant whose guilt was obvious to the prosecutors was convicted and sent to prison. Defense attorneys will argue that truth lost out. They may be right, because the jury never learned that the government's crucial witness was lying through his teeth about facts that might have undercut his credibility in the eyes of the jury. Thus, at different levels of truth, it can rightly be said that the search for truth was served and not served at the same time.

There are yet other levels of truth in a criminal case. Consider the exclusionary rule, under which truthful evidence of guilt may be kept out of a criminal trial because the police obtained it in violation of the Constitution. In most cases involving that rule, the ultimate "truth" is that the defendant is guilty. At the next level of "truth," the physical evidence seized from him is demonstrably true. But at the third level, in many such cases the police lie about the circumstances under which they secured the evidence.

Consider the following paradigmatic case. The police suspect a man who often hangs around a high school of selling heroin to kids. They have no probable cause, but they do have a good hunch that the man is a big-time dealer. They approach and grab him. One policeman reaches into the suspect's pocket and pulls out a supply of heroin packaged in small glassine envelopes of the sort that are being sold to the kids. They've got their man; now they have to make it stick. Believing more strongly in their duty to protect high school kids from heroin than in their duty to protect drug dealers from an illegal search, the police resort to a familiar "white lie"; they tell the prosecutor that the drug dealer dropped the drugs on the ground when he saw the police approaching him. The prosecutor has heard this before. It has become so familiar it even has a name: "dropsy testimony." He suspects that the search did not happen exactly as the police described it, but he cannot be absolutely certain. After all, some dealers do try to get rid of the drugs when they are about to be arrested. What is the prosecutor to do? Should he go with his suspicions, or with his loyalties to the police?

Many prosecutors will allow the police to tell their story under oath, confident that the trial judge will always believe the policeman in a one-on-one (or two-on-one) swearing contest with a drug dealer.[2]

The prosecutor also knows that the defendant will probably take the stand at the suppression hearing and lie though his teeth. He may claim that the police threatened him, that he was nowhere near the high school when he was stopped and perhaps that the police planted the drugs on him.

Somewhere along the line, the prosecutor will probably think something like this: "The defense attorney knows that his client is going to lie, yet he has no scruples about putting him on the stand. Why should I have to exact a higher standard from myself, especially since everybody knows the S.O.B. is guilty? Of course I would never deliberately suborn perjury, if I knew for certain the policeman was lying. But I only have a suspicion. So I am going to go with the cops' testimony."

It is far easier for a prosecutor to rationalize engaging in questionable conduct when he knows that the defense attorney — his opponent in the adversarial process — is entirely free to engage in analogous behavior. And therein lies the key — in my view — to *why* prosecutors engage in misconduct. They often find it difficult to understand why defense attorneys are free to do things that they are forbidden to do.

On a more subtle yet perhaps equally important level, prosecutors often fail to notice that they are coming close to the line, because defense attorneys commonly go so far over the same or an analogous line. As I will show in the next chapter, this is not a good excuse.

29

The Difference Between a Prosecutor and a Defense Attorney

Prosecutors often fail to understand that their ethical obligations are very different from those of the defense attorney. This is particularly true in the complex area of disclosure obligations. Defense attorneys are not obligated — with some very limited exceptions — to disclose incriminating information to the prosecutors. Nor are they obligated to disclose information that might impeach the credibility of defense witnesses.[1] Prosecutors, on the other hand, are obliged to disclose evidence that may help the defendant prove his innocence, reduce his sentence or cross-examine a prosecution witness. In making the difficult and often subjective judgment of whether an item of information is helpful to the defense, many prosecutors resolve doubts against disclosure. They behave in an adversarial manner, reacting to what many of them perceive as unfairness in the absence of reciprocal obligations on the part of the defense. Of course, if these prosecutors paused to think about the *reason* why they are, and the defense attorneys are not, obliged to make such disclosures, they would understand that these reasons are entirely consistent with the differing roles of the prosecutor and defense attorney in our adversary system.[2] But in the heat of a bitterly contested case, in which the defendant is obviously guilty and the defense attorney is perceived as "playing games," it is easy to understand how an honest prosecutor can come to believe that nondisclosure of material helpful to the defense will *serve* the interest of truth. This is especially true since this information will be "misused" by the defense attorney to persuade a jury that a truth-telling witness may be lying.

One of the primary reasons why otherwise honest prosecutors engage in certain kinds of misbehavior can be summarized in two words: "defense attorneys." Since defense attorneys are permitted — indeed perhaps even obliged — to go right up to the line in aggressively defending their clients, prosecutors often feel comfortable getting closer to the line than they are supposed to do.

It is important for the courts, scholars, bar associations and press to keep reminding prosecutors that they must comply with an entirely different set of standards than those applicable to the defense bar. It must be realized that the American system of criminal justice is a *modified* adversarial system: The defense attorney comes close to being a pure one-sided advocate for his generally guilty client. His job — when his client is guilty — is to prevent, by all lawful and ethical means, the "whole truth" from coming out. He is not concerned about "justice" for the general public or about the rights of victims. He is supposed to try to get his guilty client the best deal possible, preferably an acquittal.[3]

The prosecutor, on the other hand, is not supposed to prosecute a defendant who he believes is innocent. He is supposed to ensure that the truth — at each of the different levels described above — emerges. He may not employ the kinds of sharp tactics appropriate (if not always effective) to the defense. He may never place a witness, whom he believes to be lying, on the witness stand. He should resolve ethical issues in favor of doing justice rather than winning.

In brief, the prosecutor is supposed to help the defendant — in a variety of ways — to secure an acquittal, especially by providing him with useful evidence; whereas the defense attorney rarely, if ever, is supposed to help the prosecutor secure a conviction.

Until prosecutors learn — or are taught by the courts — that it is not enough for them to be "as fair" as their adversaries are, prosecutorial misconduct is likely to continue. And so long as prosecutorial misconduct persists, defense attorneys must develop both defensive and offensive counterstrategies for the benefit of their clients. When a defense attorney is representing a guilty defendant, his best friend may be a misbehaving prosecutor. Every defense attorney must learn not only how to defend against prosecutorial misconduct, but also how to turn it to the advantage of his client.

Having said all of this about some prosecutors, let me add that there are few higher callings than an honest prosecutor with a real sense of justice. Such a prosecutor can have a greater impact on the criminal justice system than any defense lawyer or judge, since most prosecutorial decisions are highly discretionary. I tell my students that if they really want to be do-gooders in the criminal justice system, they should become prosecutors who care about justice. I invite such prosecutors, past and present, to my classes as role models. For example, Stephen Trott, now a judge, speaks to my students every year about the challenges of being an honest and effective prosecutor. He served as one for most of his career. Now that he is a federal appellate court judge, he is particularly tough on young prosecutors who break the law or turn sharp corners. A good prosecutor can probably help an innocent defendant more effectively than most defense attorneys can, by insisting that the evidence be solid and that the police and prosecutors comply with their ethical obligations. A decent prosecutor can also help a guilty defendant, by exercising discretion to charge him with an appropriate crime and to seek a reasonable sentence. But because not all prosecutors are decent, we will always need zealous defense attorneys to keep prosecutors in check.

30
Lawyers' Morals — and Other Oxymorons

A *New York Times* review of one of my novels included the following words of "praise": "A fun romp with Alan Dershowitz, [*The Advocate's Devil*] gives the reader a dazzling, often rather graphic, portrayal of that greatest of all oxymorons, legal ethics. . . ." Despite the bad rap that lawyers get for being amoral, even immoral, the reality is that no profession obsesses more about morality and ethics than the legal profession. We draft codes, we teach classes, we require examination, we have ethics committees and we actually discipline and disbar — though not enough — for failure to comply with these generally high standards. That is not to deny that many lawyers run afoul of these high standards for venal or other self-serving reasons. But the reason we are so obsessed with morality is precisely that the morality of the legal profession must necessarily be situational and role-based. Acting in a representational capacity, we are required to do that which we would never do in our own private lives and that others would not be permitted to do as ordinary citizens.

We certainly don't have a license to lie or steal — indeed we have an obligation to do neither — but we do have a license to keep deep dark secrets that the public would benefit from learning. We do have a license to advocate outcomes, which we know would be objectively unjust but subjectively beneficial to our clients. In this regard, the end does justify the means, so long as the means are not themselves improper. But what is a "proper" — or, more precisely, "not improper" — means toward achieving an unjust end? For example, may an ethical lawyer cross-examine an adverse witness who he knows is telling the truth? The classic law school hypothetical involves the nearsighted bank teller who has identified your client as the bank robber. In court, she is wearing thick glasses, but your client, who has confided to you that he was the robber, remembers that the teller was not wearing glasses when she saw him. Can you ask her whether she needs glasses? Whether she was wearing them at the time in question? If she answers truthfully, can you argue, in your closing argument to the jury, that the jury should not convict a presumptively innocent defendant on the basis of the eyewitness identification of a nearsighted woman who wasn't wearing her glasses — even though you know her identification was correct?

You're not lying. Every word you have said is true. Yet you are asking the jurors to reach the wrong result.

These are the sorts of hypotheticals over which law students and lawyers obsess.

Nor are they only hypotheticals. They occur in real life with some frequency.

In my first real courtroom case, I confronted a situation that was far more difficult than the hypothetical. I was representing, on a pro bono basis, a young man who was a member of the Jewish Defense League in a case in which a bomb he had constructed killed a woman. My client had told me he had been promised by a police officer that if he disclosed who had planted the bomb he had made, he would not be prosecuted or called as a witness. When I told him that I didn't believe a policeman would make that kind of a promise, he told me he "had the cop on tape." He had surreptitiously recorded many of his conversations with the police officer. I asked him to play the tapes, and sure enough, there were several promises not to prosecute or call my client as a witness if he provided information about *other* crimes being perpetrated by the JDL. But my client did not have a tape of his conversation with the policeman about *this* crime. He said that the conversation about the other crimes had taken place in his car, which he had outfitted with a hidden tape recorder, but that the conversation about this crime took place outdoors, where he could not tape it. The existing tapes corroborated his story and I believed him, but I knew the judge would never believe his word against the word of a policeman. I had to get the policeman to admit that he had also made the promise about this case.

The only possible tactic that could produce such an admission would be to mislead the policeman into believing that we had a tape of him making the promise in regard to this case. I believed he had, in fact, made the promise. We had no tape to prove it, but the policeman didn't know that. And so, after much soul-searching and consultation with experts, I decided on the following three-part cross-examination.

First, I asked him a series of questions about promises in general without alerting him to the existence of any tapes. He lied through his teeth, repeatedly denying that he had made promises (and threats) that *were* on the tapes.

Second, I asked him whether his recollections might be refreshed by my repeating certain conversations, which I then proceeded to read from what appeared to be a transcript of a tape recording. It was, in fact, the transcript of the actual tapes. Realizing that my client had surreptiously tape-recorded him, he began to worry that he had been caught in a perjury trap. He vacillated about his prior testimony and admitted that he had made some of the promises he had earlier denied. Now it was time to spring the real trap.

Third, without missing a beat, I continue to read from what appeared to be a tape transcript. But now I was reading from a transcript of what my client told me he had been promised in regard to this crime. There was no tape of this promise, but my intention was to mislead the police officer into believing there was a tape, so that he would tell the truth. He did tell the truth, admitting that he had made the promise in regard to this crime, too.

When the judge learned that there was no tape of this promise, he hit the roof:

> THE COURT Now, I want to suggest to you, sir, that in this court, at least, one expects lawyers to keep their punches above the belt . . .
> MR. DERSHOWITZ Your Honor, I do not think there were any punches below the belt.
> THE COURT You and I then, sir, have two different ideas of the level at which one practices law . . .
> MR. DERSHOWITZ I just don't understand your argument, Your Honor.
> THE COURT Don't get the idea I am arguing with you, sir. I am expressing the opinion of the Court.
> MR. DERSHOWITZ If, in fact, he testified one way, thinking there were no tapes, and testified another, thinking there were tapes, I don't understand how anything but truth has been searched [out].
> THE COURT Is your view that you can ask questions that were, in fact, taken from a wiretap or a tape recording and in the middle of real questions, for instance, make up a little question which you slip in there, which never existed. . . .

MR. DERSHOWITZ When you say "never existed," are you suggesting made up?
THE COURT Yes.
MR. DERSHOWITZ No, that would not be proper. If you are asking whether it would be proper in the middle of conversations, which the witness assumed were on tape, to ask him about conversations which we believe occurred, but which were not recorded on tape, most affirmatively yes.
THE COURT Indicating by your actions, mannerisms, readings and other attitudes in the courtroom that it was on tape?
MR. DERSHOWITZ By all means, yes.
THE COURT You and I have a diametrically different view.
MR. DERSHOWITZ I guess we do, Your Honor.
THE COURT I regard it as a reprehensible practice.
MR. DERSHOWITZ If you would explain to me —
The COURT I am not in the business of answering questions. You do understand that, don't you?
MR. DERSHOWITZ I do not understand what is wrong with that in any way.
THE COURT I can't help you, then.

Several days later we returned to court armed with a memorandum on the propriety of the cross-examination technique used against the policeman. It cited numerous legal authorities in support of the proposition that it "has long been regarded as the essence of effective cross-examination, especially of a lying witness, to convey the impression that the cross-examiner has more, less, or different evidence than he actually has." The brief cited numerous examples similar to those used against Parola that were regarded by the authorities as "classic" instances of effective cross-examination.

We had even discovered that Abraham Lincoln, as a trial lawyer in Illinois, reputedly used a tactic not so different from ours. Francis Wellman, in his classic treatise on *The Art of Cross-Examination*, gives the following "instructive example of cross-examination": A man named Grayson was charged with murder, and his mother engaged young Abraham Lincoln to defend him. Lincoln asked an alleged eyewitness how he had observed the crime. "By moonlight," he answered. Lincoln then removed an almanac from his pocket and read that there was no moon on the night in question. Believing himself trapped by the almanac, the witness broke down and confessed to being the killer. Wellman then recounts the rumor "frequently stated by members on the Illinois circuit to this day . . . that Lincoln played a trick . . . by substituting an old calendar for the one of the year of the murder."[1]

The judge finally relented and called me into his chambers for an informal talk.

With an avuncular smile he assured me that he would not have gotten so upset at my cross-examination if I had been some "ordinary street lawyer." "But you're a Harvard law professor. You teach law students. I have to hold you to a higher standard of ethics."

I told the judge that "if I were to impose on myself what you call 'a higher standard of ethics,' then I would be imposing on my clients a lower standard of advocacy. That wouldn't be good law or good ethics. I propose to continue to resolve all ethical doubts in favor of my client and to continue to teach my students to do that if they become defense attorneys."

The judge's behavior toward me during the remainder of the hearing was exemplary.

Eventually the court of appeals, while ruling in favor of my client, went out of its way to praise my cross-examination, saying that I had "explored complex factual and legal issues competitively and yet courteously and always in the pursuit of truth." My tactics had been vindicated, but I remain troubled to this day over whether I had done the right thing.

My son, Jamin, who was a legal aid lawyer, also remains troubled over whether he did the right thing in one of his first cases. He was representing a man accused of ripping a gold chain off the neck of another man outside an after hours club. The victim himself could not identify the perp, but another man picked out my son's client. My son's investigation revealed that the man who made the identification was not a stranger who just happened to be there. He was the victim's lover. It is always relevant to cross-examine a witness about possible bias growing out of a close relationship to the victim. For example, if a woman were the witness and she was married to, or intimate with, the victim, it would not only be acceptable — it would be obligatory — to question the witness about possible bias. But the witness here was not a woman. He was another man — and he was gay, as was the victim. My son worried that if the jurors found out that the victim and the witness were gay, they might be less sympathetic to the victim and more prone to disbelieve the witness. This was more than a decade ago, and homophobia was more prevalent among jurors than it probably is today.

I told Jamin that he had no choice but to cross-examine the eyewitness with the same vigor he would employ in a heterosexual context. He came to the same conclusions, and reluctantly, he did so — and he had been bothered about it since.

Good lawyers remain obsessed with these conflicts between legal ethics (which requires zealous advocacy on behalf of clients — innocent or guilty) and personal morality (which requires decency and honesty in all dealings). There are no perfect resolutions to these and other conflicts. An effective lawyer must do everything on behalf of his client that is not forbidden by the law or the rules of the legal profession. But a good person should always be uncomfortable about doing anything that does not meet his or her personal standards of morality. The process of debating, refining and revisiting is ongoing.

If you are a decent and thinking person, you will never grow entirely comfortable with some of the tactics you will be required to employ as an effective and ethical lawyer.

31
Know When to Fight — and When to Give In

The toughest thing for a zealous lawyer to do is to give in, especially when you believe the other side is wrong. But knowing when to offer a tactical surrender can be an important part of advocacy. Don't let your ego — or even your sense of ultimate right and wrong — push you into making the wrong decision for your client.

Sometimes the option of surrender is clear. For example, if you are representing a defendant who has been denied bail, whose trial is six months off and whose prosecutor has just offered you a deal for time served, you should probably recommend accepting it, even if you believe your client may be innocent. If he goes to trial and is found guilty, he could serve an additional five years. Absent collateral consequences from a guilty plea, such as losing a job or a civil suit, it's a no-brainer. The system that creates such disincentives to going to trial — to exercising an important constitutional right — is terrible. And as a private citizen, you should be trying to change it. But as a lawyer for a client in jail, you must look out only for your client's best interest, and if his best interest is served by a guilty plea, that's what you should advise him to do — regardless of what your ego wants.

A striking example of a prominent lawyer's failure to act on this principle occurred in the case involving former president Bill Clinton. He was sued by Paula Jones in a case he believed had no merit. When settlement talks broke down, Clinton submitted to a wide-ranging deposition about his sex life. This deposition eventually resulted in Clinton's impeachment and his suspension from the practice of law. He could have avoided giving a deposition if he had simply defaulted in the Paula Jones case. Yet his lawyer, Robert Bennett, never even advised him of that option. To default would have meant to "lose" the biggest and most highly publicized case in Bennett's career. Instead, he "won" that case (at least initially — Clinton eventually had to pay more than it would have cost him to default). But that win nearly cost Clinton his presidency, his profession and even his liberty.

Learn how to surrender when losing does less harm to your client than winning.

32
Dealing with Criticism

So now you've become a successful lawyer. You're making money. You have a good client base. You're even getting some positive publicity. Life is looking up. Suddenly, the local newspaper decides to publish a critical profile of you. They get the basic facts right, but they draw all possible negative inferences against you. Anyone who doesn't know you would come away from the article thinking you are an awful person. Your friends and family are outraged by the article because they don't recognize you in its negative characterizations. Welcome to the real world of the high-profile lawyer.

How should you react to public criticism, especially criticism that is personal and that attacks your character? Should you care? Should you respond? Should you laugh it off? No matter how many times you are criticized, it always stings — at least a little bit.

Everybody has a thin skin when it comes to personal attack. But over the years, my own skin has thickened somewhat — perhaps because of all the calluses that have resulted from the multiplicity of attacks — and I think I have learned how to deal with the public criticism that comes along with the job. At least it works for me.

The first rule is to distinguish between criticism by people who know you and criticism by strangers. I take very seriously all criticisms from my friends, colleagues, family members, and people I care about. I am fortunate to have friends and family who are willing to tell me when they disagree with me or when they don't like something I'm doing. These people know me well, understand me and care about me. Their criticism is entirely valid. Strangers, on the other hand, have no idea who I am. They may see me on television, but as my wife always tells me, "That's not you on TV; that's 'talk-bite Dersh.'"

The second rule is never to take public *praise* too seriously if it comes from strangers. If you're not going to take the criticism of strangers seriously, then you can't have a different standard for accepting public praise by strangers. I know lots of people who live for public praise by strangers, and then are devastated by public criticism. Recently, a friend of mine received a bad review for a film he had produced. The reviewer was someone he had never heard of, yet he was devastated. I asked him what he would think if a stranger walked up to him on the street and told him he didn't like the film. He said he would ignore such criticism. The criticism he received from a reviewer was more damaging because it was widely read by others. But in terms of his own feelings, it should not have made much of a difference. I cautioned him, however, that if he takes this approach, he must also ignore positive reviews from strangers. You can't have it both ways.

This symmetrical approach — applying the same standard to public praise and public criticism — is particularly important for lawyers who represent controversial clients. The public will love you when your client is popular and hate you when he is unpopular. Shortly after the Simpson case, a Jewish woman approached me on the street and told me that she used to love me when I represented people like Anatoly Sharansky (the Soviet dissident) and Jonathan Pollard (the American Jew who spied for Israel), but she had lost all respect for me when I agreed to represent O. J. Simpson. I told her she was wrong for liking me *or* disliking me on the basis of my clients. Later that same day, an African-American expressed love for me because I had represented Simpson. I replied, "Don't love me, because tomorrow you're going to hate me for representing some racist you despise."

It's important not to live and die by the fickle reviews or assessments of strangers. That doesn't mean you should ignore them. I certainly don't. I correct the record whenever I am made aware of a false statement made about me, because otherwise it will be repeated and become part of the public record (especially with computer research). But I try not to let public criticism get to me personally — unless, of course, it's well founded.

Part THREE

Being a Good Person

33

Can a Good Lawyer Be a Good Person?

To the question "Are lawyers vilified too much or not enough?" my standard answer is "yes." Some lawyers, who deserve praise for their selfless efforts on behalf of the disenfranchised, are unjustly vilified. Others, who deserve vilification for their self-serving assistance of the exploitatively powerful, are unjustly honored.

Most of the rest of us deserve a mixture of praise, vilification and benign neglect for our mixed clientele and practices. The important point is that, far too often, lawyers are attacked for the wrong reasons.

Whenever I appear on talk shows, I am criticized for representing guilty clients. "How can you sleep at night," I am asked, "when you help someone who you know is guilty get back on the street?" Replying that I'm part of an adversarial system barely satisfies an audience fearful of crime and fed up with what it perceives as legal gamesmanship.

Somewhat more surprising is the widespread criticism directed against personal injury lawyers who "sue too much." It is understandable why these so-called ambulance chasers would be unpopular with insurance companies, large consumer-oriented businesses and some governmental entities. But why should the average wage earner — who is far more likely to be a plaintiff than a defendant in a contingency-fee, personal injury or breach-of-warranty case — be so upset at private lawyers who compete with ambulance-chasing claim agents sent out to secure settlements favorable to the insurance companies? Plaintiffs' lawyers help level the playing field against large insurance companies. The fact that they do it out of self-serving profit motives is simply part of the free-market world in which the legal profession functions.

To be sure, the contingency fee, which is an evil made necessary by the inability of most personal injury plaintiffs to afford legal fees prior to recovering damages, is often abused, especially in open-and-shut cases, where the only real issue is monetary damages.

Indigent plaintiffs do have a legitimate grievance against lawyers who keep too much of the judgment or settlement for themselves. But defendants have little legitimate standing to complain about contingency-fee lawyers. And the average member of the public should have little antagonism toward them.

Nor do I understand the widespread public complaints about lawyers who advertise or who "stir up litigation." On a recent television show, Walter Olson and I debated this issue. Olson pointed to ads in which lawyers urge spouses to consider breaking up their marriage. I have never seen such an ad, nor would it be very effective. I have seen ads urging parents of children born with birth defects to consult a lawyer about possible medical malpractice.

On balance, I think that probably does more good than harm. If, in fact, malpractice does contribute to some birth defects, as it surely does, then those potential plaintiffs least likely to be aware of their rights should be alerted to the possibility that they may have a claim.

If it turns out that their claim is weak or nonexistent, the market effect of the contingency-fee mechanism will likely prevent a lawsuit. (It can be argued that the substantive law should not recognize claims in which justice and science fail to support liability, but that is an argument for change in the substantive law, not for an attack on the messenger, in this case the personal injury lawyer.)

The argument made by Olson and others is that litigation costs are passed on to all consumers. But that begs the important questions: Does increased litigation help secure just compensation for injured plaintiffs? Does it improve the safety of products? Does it decrease malpractice? If it does, then these costs should be shared by all consumers, just as the direct costs of preventing negligence are shared.

It is ironic that those who most loudly proclaim the virtues of the free market are often the most vocal opponents of free-market mechanisms when it comes to personal injury litigation and self-regulation of lawyers. That is because these hypocrites do not really favor a neutral free market when it hurts their own pocketbooks — only when it helps.

More lawsuits may not be good for large corporations, but they are good for justice and society, especially if brought by the powerless against the powerful. Obviously any virtue taken to excess may become a vice. There certainly are too many frivolous lawsuits, just as there are too many frivolous defenses of valid claims. These excesses can be controlled by reasonable rules that operate neutrally to favor neither the powerless nor the powerful.

But a knee-jerk, blanket condemnation of more litigation is not neutral; it favors the rich, the powerful and the exploiters over the poor, the powerless and the victims.

Some of the most commendable lawyers in history have been high-level ambulance chasers who have stirred up litigation by making disenfranchised people aware of their legal rights. Public interest lawyers such as Ralph Nader, Thurgood Marshall, Clarence Darrow and Morris Dees have encouraged lethargic, frightened, untutored and indigent plaintiffs to demand their rights. Even Judge Joseph Wapner, of TV's *People's Court*, had the show's host urge his millions of viewers to "take 'em to court" if they believe they have a legitimate grievance.

It may seem like a stretch to put the local personal injury lawyer who buys time on late-night TV in the same category as these selfless legal luminaries. But both types of ambulance chasing achieve a similar result: more litigation by people who would not otherwise have known that they had a right to redress their grievances in a court of law.

Opponents of the so-called litigation explosion — and there is some doubt whether there has, in fact, been an explosion — often point to countries like Japan, which have far fewer lawyers and lawsuits. But in most such places, victims of corporate and governmental negligence and malfeasance passively take it, rather than fighting back in court. That, for better or worse, is not the American way. It has not been the American way since de Tocqueville wrote about our new nation more than a century ago. So let's hear two-and-a-half cheers for ambulance chasers, barators and other assorted legal troublemakers. They do a lot more good for justice, equality and safety — for society in general — than many of their more respected brothers and sisters at the bar, who quietly work long and well-compensated hours in the *pro malo publico* defense of negligent (sometimes quite deliberate) tortfeasors, warranty breachers, environmental polluters and other assorted do-badders.

These are the lawyers who are not vilified enough. They continue to be honored both within and without the bar. To be sure, every defendant is entitled to a defense, but that canon of the law is more compelling in the criminal context, where the power of government is brought to bear on an individual, than it is in the context of a corporation that is being sued by an indigent victim for creating unsafe or polluting conditions. Indeed, even in the context of criminal cases, no ongoing criminal organization is entitled to have house counsel — a consigliere — who helps it continue in its criminal ways.

Yet many civil lawyers do assist large businesses in continuing their profitable negligence and unsafe practices. Consider, for example, the legion of high-priced lawyers who make a living defending the cigarette industry. Unlike other products that do some good but also create risks, cigarettes do only harm. Tobacco kills and injures more people — some smokers started as teens who were seduced by deliberately false advertising claims that made cigarettes seem like a health product in the 1940s — each year than all the violent felonies combined. Not only do cigarettes kill smokers, but we now know that they injure nonsmokers. No objective, rational person can doubt that there is a close relationship between cigarette smoking and various diseases. Yet these lawyers — some from the most prestigious firms in our nation — use every legal device at their vast disposal to bludgeon plaintiffs who are dying of cigarette-related cancer and emphysema. These lawyers are not vilified but honored, which makes no sense, except that we generally honor wealth, success and status — attributes that come with the territory of representing large tobacco companies.

I could give many more examples, although perhaps none as clear-cut as the cigarette defense bar, of those who do dishonorable work. The point is, if you do it with distinction, without fanfare and with a cum laude degree from an elite law school, few questions will be asked about the social utility of what is being done. The bottom line is that the current attack on lawyers is not neutral or value-free. It is a well-orchestrated campaign conducted by business interests that have the most to lose from increased litigation. If it succeeds, it will return the playing field to the unlevel condition it was in before people began to take their rights seriously. No one who cares about justice should fall for the slogans in this campaign against the litigation explosion. There are important steps that can and should be taken to reduce the expenses, abuses, misuses and excesses of the present system. More efficient and less expensive and time-consuming methods of alternative dispute resolution should be introduced. The contingency fee should be regulated so as not to permit windfalls to plaintiffs' lawyers in open-and-shut cases. Sanctions should be permitted for, but limited to, cases that are brought or defended for harassment purposes, with no realistic expectation of prevailing on the merits.

Finally, we should continue to vilify lawyers who deserve vilification, and to honor lawyers who merit honor, but we must be sure we know which is which.

34

Can You Pass the "Fluoridation" Test?

So you want to become a personal injury lawyer — a tort lawyer. That certainly is where the really big money is. The only lawyers whose yearly incomes are in nine figures — that means more than $100 million a year — are tort lawyers. Certainly not all or even most tort lawyers, but a significant number, make eight- and nine-figure incomes. This has been especially so since the cigarette industry began to settle statewide cases. Recently I helped three Florida lawyers secure the right to a ten-figure legal fee in a cigarette case that they helped settle for an eleven-figure sum! (The billionaire Florida lawyers tried to stiff me on my tiny fee, but they finally settled the matter.)

The amount of money some of these lawyers make is staggering. Calculated on an hourly basis, their fees come to tens of thousands of dollars an hour. And some of them are relatively mediocre lawyers who do little more than help to get the business by knowing the right politicians. Others work hard and do good. They also take risks, because their fees are contingent on winning — or settling. If their clients get nothing, they get nothing. But they know that going in, and so they rarely take a case unless they are assured of a high likelihood of winning at least something.

If you decide to become a tort lawyer, you should constantly ask yourself what I call the "Fluoridation Test" question. When I was a kid, there was a debate over whether the drinking water should be fluoridated to reduce the number of dental cavities, especially in children. Most dentists, being decent people, favored fluoridation, even though they knew it would be bad for business. After all, fewer cavities means fewer fillings and billings. Some selfish dentists, however, put their own pocketbook interest before the dental health of their patients — and people in general. They came up with all sorts of rationalizations — medical, political and economic (my particular favorite was the local dentist who told one of my relatives that it was important for kids to have some cavities so that they had to go to the dentist, who can then spot more serious problems).

How does the fluoride test question relate to the morality of personal injury lawyers? They have to ask themselves an analogous question whenever a proposal is made that will help their clients and people in general, but at some personal cost to them. The National Association of Criminal Lawyers, for example, strongly advocates decriminalization of many drug crimes, the abolition of the death penalty, the broadening of legal aid and other changes that will cost many criminal lawyers a significant amount of business. They pass the fluoridation test with flying colors. The American Trial Lawyers Association, which is the trade organization for personal injury lawyers, has not been active in promoting reforms that do not line their own pockets. They, too, rationalize their opposition to all changes that threaten their pocketbooks by arguing that what is good for them is also good for their clients. Well, maybe most of the time, but certainly not all of the time. Contingency fees come out of the pockets of their clients. There are some proposed reforms that would clearly benefit clients at the expense of their lawyers. Decent lawyers should favor these reforms.

35
Graduating Law Students

You are graduating at a time of wonderful opportunity and challenge. Now a caution sign! You're entering into an ethically treacherous profession. The danger points are generally unmarked, sometimes even mismarked. The potential for corruption will be ever present, and you will see — as Ecclesiastes before you saw — the unrighteous rewarded and the righteous punished. You will see subtle forms of elite cheating all around you and be tempted to join in, because the rewards are very high and the risks fairly low. For many, it becomes a way of life — business as usual — and they accept it without even thinking about it. It begins right after law school graduation. If you are a law clerk, you will see judges distorting the facts and the law, playing favorites with lawyers and rendering result-oriented decisions reflecting their politics, ambitions and prejudices. Because you will like your judge, you may blind yourself to what he or she is doing. Or worse, incorporate their ethics into your own. If you are a prosecutor in the best of offices, you will see some of your seniors subtly pushing perjuring policemen toward even better perjury, or neglecting their Brady obligations. If you are a defense attorney, you will see colleagues overpreparing witnesses and overselling their personal relationships with prosecutors and judges. If you go to a law firm, you will hear about partners overbilling and charging for hours during which they were doing other things. You will attend bar association tributes to ethically questionable lawyers, and you will see honest lawyers fired or losing clients because they are regarded as insufficiently aggressive. Now is the time for you to choose whether you will accept ethical compromise in order to maximize your success.

What kind of lawyer will you become? Will you go along with this form of pervasive cheat elite? Or will you live by your own higher internal standards of personal and professional morality? You must make a choice. It is not optional. You cannot remain passive. You must commit. Will you accept the Faustian bargain or resist? Many lawyers, unlike Faust, never make an explicit choice. They simply drift toward a widely accepted form of elite corruption without ever engaging in the "to be or not to be" soliloquy. Most lawyers who cross the line into corruption do not make an explicit decision to become corrupt. They do not make a deliberate and calculating step over the line. They move closer and closer until they realize — and sometimes they never realize — that the line is well behind them.

Part of the problem is that many of the lines are anything but clear. They are kept deliberately vague in order to vest maximum discretion in disciplinary committees and courts. Another related problem is that only a small percentage of corrupt lawyers are caught — in the way that Web Hubbell, for example, was caught and disgraced. The very fact that Hubbell was willing to risk the scrutiny he had to know his high position at the Justice Department would subject him to — knowing he had overbilled his clients and his firm — shows how unlikely he thought it would be that he would ever be caught and prosecuted.

The tragedy is that a cost-benefit analysis may well lead to a life of elite corruption, of becoming the kind of successful lawyer whose main tools are not law books, but telephone books and checkbooks. Roy Cohen famously said, “I don’t care if my opponent knows the law, as long as I know the judge.” Most of today’s corrupt lawyers are not as blatant, but they believe — and they tell potential clients — how close they are to the judge or the prosecutor who will decide their fate. And the problem is, they might be right, at least with regard to some judges and prosecutors. I have seen it, and so have many others.

One of the greatest judges in history understood corruption since he saw it up close and personal: His father was corrupt. Benjamin Cardozo dedicated his own life to resisting corruption — to living a professional life of pure law. He decided. He didn’t drift. He knew what kind of a lawyer — and person — he wanted to be. He became a judge. In one sense, it's far simpler to be an ethical and moral judge, without compromising any principles, than to be, for example, a criminal defense lawyer who never compromises with personal morality.

Criminal defense lawyers are ethically obliged to go right up to the line of legally and ethically permissible conduct in the interests of their clients. To withhold a permissible, tactical benefit from a criminal defendant because you — his lawyer — feel morally uncomfortable about employing it is to deny him his constitutional right to a zealous representation. For example, you *must* cross-examine an incriminating eyewitness whose identification is subject to effective impeachment, even if you know — because your client told you in confidence — that the witness is telling the truth. You *must* invoke exclusionary rules to keep the jury from hearing inculpatory evidence you know will make the difference between convicting and acquitting a guilty murderer — who may kill again. You have a license *not to lie*, but to try to produce factually false verdicts, so long as you do so by ethically permissible means.

But many young lawyers fail to understand the limitations of this dangerous license and that it extends *only* to the defense of others. It does not extend to personal or professional decisions about your own life. When you are not acting in a representational capacity, you have no license to go right up to the line or employ an end-justifies-the-means calculus.

Indeed, too many lawyers reverse the moral calculus: They turn the salutory principle of zealous advocacy for others on its head. They are insufficiently zealous in the defense of others, and overly aggressive in support of their own financial ends.

Deuteronomy commands, "Justice, justice shall you pursue." Commentators ask why the word "justice" is repeated. My own interpretation is to teach that justice has a different meaning when you are acting for others and for yourself.

Prepare ahead of time for ethical conflicts. Cheats tend to be charming and seductive. Know your own values. The Code of Professional Responsibility will not resolve all of your conflicts. You must, of course, obey them, but they are minimal standards.

Think through your own standards.

Dream bold dreams.

Do great things.

Always remember Hillel's second admonition:

If I am for myself alone,
What am I?

36
Graduating University Students

Nearly forty years ago, I sat out there in a place much like this, surrounded by proud and frightened family members. Proud because I — like so many in my class and so many in your class — was the first in my immediate family to graduate from college and law school. Frightened, because our family knew that in order to get the excellent education we were given, we had been asked — subtly to be sure, but asked nonetheless — to make a Faustian pact with a twentieth-century American devil. The bargain was this: In exchange for being taught by some of the finest professors in the world, I was expected to reject my tradition, my ethnicity, my religious background and my heritage. This was asked not only of me and of my co-religionists, but also of my African-American classmates, my Irish-American classmates, my Italian-American classmates, my Hispanic-American classmates and all of the rest of our largely hyphenated class. It was asked of us for the best of motives. Part of the college's and law school's mission in those days was to Americanize us, to assimilate us, to homogenize us. It was as if the Eleventh Commandment and the Twenty-fifth Amendment read: "Thou shalt melt into the great melting pot called America and become more like the 'real' Americans who founded this great nation." And many did melt. Names and noses were both shortened. Accents and mannerisms were refined. We learned to wear tweed and we tried to smoke pipes.

Some of us kept our noses and names. Recently, a prominent politician who had read my book *Chutzpah* told me about a situation that was parallel in his life and in mine. He, too, graduated from law school and was, like me, turned down by every single Wall Street law firm to which he applied. He was told by his dean that he'd better change his name. And he went home that night and made a list of possible names and finally came up with "Mark Conrad." And then he looked at himself in the mirror and said, "I'm no Mark Conrad. I'm Mario Cuomo, and I'm gonna stay that way!"

The paragraph to which he was referring in my book told about a dream I used to have during my first years of teaching at Harvard. In the dream, I was standing in the middle of Harvard yard, between my mother and Derek Bok, then president of Harvard. Both looked at me and they saw two completely different people. Derek Bok saw me as a shtetl Jew with sidelocks and prayer shawl; my mother saw me as an assimilated WASP carrying a polo mallet. In many ways, it was the worst of all possible worlds. To our parents we had joined the "thems," abandoning our heritage; to the "thems" we were a younger version of our grandparents, still living in the ghettos.

Then the pendulum suddenly swung: Tribalism, separatism, scapegoating, name-calling, claims of superiority became the order of the day; Farrakhan, Levin, Jeffries, Kahane each preaching not only pride but prejudice and racial or religious superiority. It was pride run amok.

Calls for censorship, firing, political correctness, political incorrectness, provocations, counterprovocations filled the air. College campuses began to resemble an academic version of Beirut or Sarajevo, where people were no longer judged by the content of their character, but instead by the color of their skin, their national origin, their religion, their gender, their sexual preference and their ethnicity.

Debate raged — and continues to rage — over how much weight to give to race, ethnicity, gender and other such factors in admission and hiring decisions. Court decisions confused and compounded. Rationales were offered on all sides, but often it just came down to my immigrant grandmother's question when I told her in 1955 that the Brooklyn Dodgers had finally won the World Series: "Is that good or bad for the Jews?" Is it good or bad for my particular group? If it's good for another, it must be bad for mine. The legitimate quest for equality is not a zero-sum game!

My call to you today is to keep your pride without prejudice, ethnicity without superiority, heritage without hegemony. I believe it is possible to keep and use pride positively, without undercutting the pride of others, without blaming, without scapegoating. It's a difficult challenge. Assimilating and melting is no challenge. Nor is separating and scapegoating. But the real challenge is to remain part of one's heritage without demeaning the heritage of others.

When you leave this place for the marketplace or for public service, do not leave your heritage behind! Go forward with pride in your traditions, in your families, in your ethnicity, in your gender, in your national origin.

Keep the hyphen! It is the single most important punctuation mark in American history. President Woodrow Wilson was wrong to criticize "some Americans [who] need hyphens," as was President Theodore Roosevelt, who foolishly claimed that "the hyphen is incompatible with patriotism." It was hyphenated Americans who have made this country unique.

African-Americans, Hispanic-Americans, Asian-Americans, Arab-Americans, Italian-Americans, Russian-Americans, Greek-Americans, Irish-Americans, Women-Americans, Gay-Americans, Native-Americans, Jewish-Americans — all of these hyphenated Americans have turned this country from a nineteenth-century land with great potential into the greatest country in history.

And we are great because we are the most diverse, the most multiracial, the most multilinguistic, multiethnic, multireligious nation in the history of the world. We are all descendants of immigrants — except those

Native Americans whom our ancestors tried to destroy. Many of us are descendants of immigrants who originally came here *illegally*: My own grandfather saved dozens of our family from the Holocaust by obtaining false affidavits from nonexistent synagogues claiming they needed rabbis. The children of these illegal immigrants are now prominent educators, businesspeople and productive citizens.

Yes, we are all Americans, but each of us brings a special ingredient to the zest of our national stew. The marketplace of ideas must be open to all. For those of you who would censor in the name of political correctness, I urge you to look back to the history of the 1950s, when political correctness prevailed on campuses. But the people with the power to define what was correct in those days came from the right rather than from the left. McCarthyism was the 1950s version of today's political correctness, but far more dangerous because it carried with it the sanction of the state. We must trust neither the right nor the left with our liberties. We must have faith in the marketplace of ideas, especially on college campuses.

Let me end by telling a story that comes from my own particular tradition, my favorite story from the Talmud. It involves a class about the law of property. The teacher explained that if somebody finds a valuable bird more than fifty feet from someone's house, the bird belongs to the person who found it. But if someone finds a valuable bird within fifty feet of someone's house, it belongs to the person whose house it was found near. Young Jeremiah, a student, raised his hand and asked the following question: "But Rabbi, what if one foot of the bird is within fifty feet and one foot of the bird is outside of fifty feet? What is the rule?" And the Talmud says, "For asking that question Jeremiah was thrown out of the yeshiva."

I love that story because I went to parochial school, I used to ask those kinds of questions and I used to get thrown out. Then I went to law school and learned that every hard question has one foot of the bird on one side and one on the other side of the line. The foot of pride, the foot of prejudice, the foot of freedom of speech, the foot of bigotry. And so I urge you, as you go forward in the world, never forget your heritage and never stop asking the hard questions.

37
Why Be a Good Person?

For most people, the question "Why be good?" as distinguished from merely law-abiding is a simple one. Because God commands it, because the Bible requires it, because good people go to heaven and bad people go to hell. The vast majority of people derive their morality from religion. This is not to say that all religious people are moral or of good character — far from it. But it is easy to understand why a person who believes in a God who rewards and punishes would want to try to conform his or her conduct to God's commandments. A cost-benefit analysis should persuade any believer that the eternal costs of hell outweigh any earthly benefit to be derived by incurring the wrath of an omniscient and omnipotent God. Even the skeptic might be inclined to resolve doubts in favor of obeying religious commands. As Pascal put it more than three hundred years ago: "You must wager. It is not optional. You are embarked. . . . Let us weigh the gain and the loss in wagering that God is. Let us estimate these two chances. If you gain, you gain all; if you lose, you lose nothing. Wager, then, without hesitation that He is."

I have always considered "Pascal's Wager" as a questionable bet to place, since any God worth believing in would prefer an honest agnostic to a calculating hypocrite. To profess belief on a cost-benefit analysis is to trivialize religion. Consider, for example, the decision of Thomas More to face earthly execution rather than eternal damnation. When the king commands one action and God commands another, a believer has no choice. This is the way More reportedly put it: "The Act of Parliament is like a sword with two edges, for if a man answer one way, it will confound his soul, and if he answer the other way, it will confound his body."

More followed God's order and gave up his life on earth for the promise of eternal salvation. For his martyrdom — for his goodness — More has been accorded the honor of sainthood.

I have never quite understood why people who firmly believe they are doing God's will are regarded as "good," even "heroic." For them the choice is a tactical one that serves their own best interests, a simple consequence of a cost-benefit analysis. Thomas More seemed to understand this far better than those who have lionized him over the centuries.

To a person who believes that the soul lives forever and the body is merely temporary, it is a simple matter to choose the edge of the sword that will cut off earthly life but preserve the soul. Heaven and hell are forever, while life on earth, especially for a man of More's age, lasts only a few years. Therefore, if More truly believed in reward and punishment after life, he was no hero. By choosing death over damnation, he demonstrated nothing more than his abiding belief; giving up a few years on earth for an eternity in heaven was a wise trade-off that should earn him a place of honor in the pantheon of true believers, but not in the pantheon of heroes.

The basic question remains: Why is it more noble for a firm believer to do something because God has commanded it than because the king has, if to that person God is more powerful than any king? In general, submission to the will of a powerful person has not been regarded as especially praiseworthy, except, of course, by the powerful person. Would Thomas More have joined the genocidal crusades in the eleventh century just because God and the Pope commanded it? If he had, would he justly be regarded as a good person? Nor is this question applicable only to Christian believers. I have wondered why Jews praise Abraham for his willingness to murder his son when God commanded it. A true hero who believed in a God who rewards and punishes would have resisted that unjust command and risked God's wrath, just as a true hero would have refused God's order to murder "heathen" women and children during the barbaric Crusades.

The true hero — the truly good person — is the believer who risks an eternity in hell by refusing an unjust demand by God. The great eighteenth-century rabbi, Levi Isaac of Berdichev, was such a hero. He brought a religious lawsuit against God, and told God that he would refuse to obey any divine commands that endangered the welfare of the Jewish people. By doing so, Levi Isaac may have risked divine punishment, but he acted heroically. He stood up to a God who he believed had the power to punish him but who he also believed was acting unjustly. In challenging God, he was following the tradition of the heroic Abraham, who argued with God over His willingness to sacrifice the innocent along with the guilty of Sodom, rather than the example of the compliant Abraham, who willingly obeyed God's unjust command to sacrifice the innocent Isaac (or the ultimately compliant Job who apologized to God for doubting His justice, after God had indeed acted unjustly by killing Job's children just to prove a point to the devil).

This, then, is the conundrum of judging goodness in a religious person who believes in divine reward and punishment. Those religious leaders who select martyrs and saints cannot have it both ways. They cannot declare someone to be both a hero and a believer, because the two honors are logically inconsistent. The undoubting believer is less of a hero for choosing death over eternal damnation. The real hero is necessarily less of an undoubting believer. Real heroes are those who face death for a principle — say, to save the lives of others — without any promise of reward.

Only if More were in fact a hypocrite, feigning belief in the hereafter but really a secret disbeliever, would he deserve the status of hero, but then of course he would be denied the accolade given for true belief — and for honesty.

There is, to be sure, an intermediate position. More could have been someone who tried hard to believe but could not suppress doubt. I suspect many thinking people today are in that position. If that were the case with More, his decision to choose death entailed some degree of risk. Maybe he was giving up a bird in his earthly hand, namely what was left of his life, for two in the heavenly bush, namely a chance at a possible heaven. But this, too, would be a calculation, albeit a more complex and probabilistic one. (I am not suggesting that religious martyrs always think this way consciously, but surely they experience this mix of belief, calculation and action at some level.)

This is not to argue that believing persons cannot be truly moral. They certainly can. Perhaps they would have acted morally without the promise of reward or the threat of punishment. This is to suggest, however, that to the extent conduct is determined by such promises and rewards, it is difficult to measure its inherent moral quality as distinguished from its tactical component.

But what about atheists, agnostics or other individuals who make moral decisions without regard to any God or any promise or threat of the hereafter? Why should such people be moral? Why should they develop a good character? Why should they not simply do what is best for them?

Even the Bible provides a model for such people. The author of Ecclesiastes explicitly tells us that he (or she, since the original Hebrew word for Ecclesiastes is *Koheleth*, which means "female gatherer") does not believe in any hereafter.

I have seen everything during my vain existence, a righteous man being destroyed for all his righteousness and a sinner living long for all his wickedness.

. . . [T]he fate of men and the fate of beasts is the same. As the one dies, so does the other, for there is one spirit in both and man's distinction over the beast is nothing, for everything is vanity. All go to one place, all come from the dust and all return to the dust. Who knows whether the spirit of men rises upward and the spirit of the beast goes down to the earth?

Nor surprisingly, Ecclesiastes concludes that "there is nothing better for man than to rejoice in his words, for that is his lot, and no one can permit him to see what shall be afterwards." And Ecclesiastes goes on to recommend hedonistic selfishness as a response to the absence of a hereafter: "I know that there is no other good in life but to be happy while one lives. Indeed, every man who eats, drinks and enjoys happiness in his work — that is the gift of God."

Ecclesiastes is wrong. Even if there are no heaven and hell, there are good reasons for human beings to do better than merely be happy. The truly moral person is the one who does the right thing without any promise of reward or threat of punishment — without engaging in a cost-benefit analysis. Doing something because God has said to do it does not make a person moral: It merely tells us that person is a prudential believer, akin to the person who obeys the command of an all-powerful secular king. Abraham's willingness to sacrifice his son Isaac because God told him to does not make Abraham moral; it merely shows that he was obedient. Far too many people abdicate moral responsibility to God, as Abraham did. Accordingly, for purposes of discussing character and morality, I will assume that there is no God who commands, rewards, punishes or intervenes. Whether or not this is true — whatever "true" means in the context of faith — it is a useful heuristic device by which to assess character and morality. Just as Pascal argued that the most prudent wager is to put your eternal money on God, so, too, it is a useful construct to assume God's nonexistence when judging whether a human action should be deemed good. There is a wonderful Hasidic story about a rabbi who was asked whether it is ever proper to act as if God did not exist. He responded, "Yes, when you are asked to give to charity, you should give as if there were no God to help the object of the charity." I think the same is true of morality and character: In deciding what course of action is moral, you should act as if there were no God. You should also act as if there were no threat of earthly punishment or reward. You should be a person of good character because it is right to be such a person.

I am reminded of the cartoon depicting an older married man marooned on a deserted island with a younger woman. He asks her to have sex, arguing, "No one would ever know." The woman responds, "I would know." The "I would know" test of good character is a useful one.

What, then, is the content of good character in a world without the threat of divine or earthly punishment and without the promise of divine or earthly reward? In such a world every good act would be done simply because it was deemed by the actor to be good. Good character in such a world would involve striking an appropriate balance among often competing interests, such as the interests of oneself and of others, of the present and of the future, of one's family (tribe, race, gender, religion, nation and so forth) and of strangers. Since the beginning of time, civilized humans have struggled to achieve that golden mean. The great Rabbi Hillel put it well when he said: "If I am not for myself, who will be for me, but if I am for myself alone, what am I?"

Good character consists of recognizing the selfishness that inheres in each of us and trying to balance it against the altruism to which we should all aspire. It is a difficult balance to strike, but no definition of goodness can be complete without it.

Lawyers, perhaps more than most others, need a strong moral core because their professional terrain is so ethically ambiguous and because the temptations to take moral shortcuts are so pervasive. For some this moral core will derive from religious belief, for others from a philosophical commitment, and yet for others from the oath we take when we are admitted to the bar. Whatever its source, the moral core should serve as a constant against which professional judgments are evaluated.

Notes

Chapter 1

1. Quoted in Alschuler, Albert, *Law Without Values* (Chicago, 2000), pp. 28–29.

2. The sacrifice may really be a conflict between personal and professional principles. See Chapter 9.

3. *Supreme Injustice*, New York: Oxford University Press, 2001.

Chapter 9

1. In a recent case, a priest and a lawyer both revealed information proving the innocence of a prisoner, which had been given to them in confidence years earlier by a man who since died. See *New York Times* July 25, 2001, p. 1.

Chapter 11

1. *The Best Defense*, *Reasonable Doubts*, and *The Advocate's Devil.*

2. Michael Lerner, the editor of *Tikkun* magazine, used these words to describe me.

3. In his response, Gabel essentially conceded that under existing law — which he would change — a lawyer is obliged to defend his client zealously and raise all possible defenses. (See *Tikkun*, Sept. 19, 1997.)

Chapter 16

1. See Alan Dershowitz and John Ely, *Some Anxious Observations on the Candor and Logic of the Emerging Nixon Majority*, 80 Yale L. J. 1198 (1971).

Chapter 17

1. Following the decision in *Bush v. Gore*, I wrote an op-ed article for the *Los Angeles Times* concerning the obligation of law clerks to blow the whistle on corrupt judges. I reprint it here because it elaborates on the prior article.

Chapter 19

1. Subject, of course, to reporting requirements, etc.

Chapter 23

1. In the early 1970s, I wrote a series of articles for the *New York Times* about the confusion between judicial and political philosophy in which I made the following point: What

the President [Nixon] meant by "judicial" philosophy is far less clear. "Now I paraphrase the word 'judicial,'" he said, and "by judicial philosophy I do not mean agreeing with the President on every issue." A justice, he continued, "should not twist or bend the Constitution in order to perpetuate his political and social views." After assuring his audience that the nominees shared his judicial philosophy and that they were conservatives ("but only in a judicial, not in a political, sense"), the President went on to give an example of what a conservative judicial philosophy means to him: "As a judicial conservative, I believe that some Court decisions have gone too far in the past in weakening the peace forces as against the criminal forces in our society. The peace forces must not be denied the legal tools they need to protect the innocent from criminal elements." The President's law-and-order attitude is not a "judicial philosophy." It is just the sort of "personal political and social view" that the President emphasizes should not be perpetuated by a Supreme Court justice. A judicial philosophy deals with the roles of the Court as an institution. It is responsive to questions such as: What precedential weight should be given to prior decisions? What power should the Court exercise over the other branches of the federal government and over the states? What tools of judicial construction should it employ in giving meaning to a constitutional or statutory provision? A judicial philosophy — if it is truly judicial rather than "political" or "social" — does not speak in terms of giving the peace forces "tools" to "protect the innocent from criminal elements." A "conservative" judicial philosophy is one that respects precedent and that avoids deciding cases on constitutional ground whenever a narrower ground for a decision is available. Most importantly, a judge with a conservative judicial philosophy abjures employing the courts to effectuate his own political or social program — he is a decider of cases rather than an advocate of causes (Alan M. Dershowitz, "Of Justices and 'Philosophies,'" *New York Times*, Week in Review, Oct. 24, 1971).

2. These cases are cited in Dershowitz, *Supreme Injustice* (New York: Oxford University Press, 2001), pp. 47–48, 221–23.

Chapter 28

1. A. Dershowitz, *The Best Defense* (Random House, 1982), p. 371.

2. Here is the way one judge — then a practicing lawyer — described the dilemma he faced when confronted with such testimony: "Were this the first time a policeman had testified that a defendant dropped a packet of drugs to the ground, the matter would be unremarkable. The extraordinary thing is that each year in our criminal courts policemen give such testimony in hundreds, perhaps thousands, of cases — and that, in a nutshell, is the problem of 'dropsy' testimony. It disturbs me now, and it disturbed me when I was at the Bar. . . . Our refusal to face up to the 'dropsy' problem soils the rectitude of the administration of justice. One is tempted to deal with it now by suppressing 'dropsy' evidence out of hand; yet I cannot. Reason and settled rules of law lead the other way, and Judges serve the integrity of the means, not the attractiveness of the end." Irving Younger, cited in Goldstein, Dershowitz

and Schwartz, *Criminal Law: Theory and Practice* (New York: Free Press, 1974), pp. 484–485.

Chapter 29

1. Defense attorneys are not, however, permitted to call defense witnesses who they know will commit perjury.

2. See ABA Standards for Criminal Justice, the Prosecution Function, the Defense Function (2d ed., 1980).

3. Nor is this a transient or radical notion, as reflected by the following question from a British barrister in 1920: "An advocate, by the sacred duty which he owes his client, knows, in the discharge of that office, but one person in the world, that client and none other. To save that client by all expedient means — to protect that client at all hazards and costs to all others, and among others to himself — is the highest and most unquestioned of his duties; and he must not regard the alarm, the suffering, the torment, the destruction which he may bring upon any other. Nay, separating even the duties of a patriot from those of an advocate, and casting them, if need be, to the wind, he must go on reckless of the consequences, if his fate should unhappily be, to involve his country in confusion for his client's protection." Quoted in A. Dershowitz, *The Best Defense*, pp. xv-xvi.

Chapter 30

1. This Lincoln story, like so many others, is partly apocryphal. The actual facts appear to be as follows:

Lincoln showed the witness an almanac and asked him:

Q: Does not the almanac say that on August 29 the moon was barely past the first quarter instead of being full?

A: (No answer.)

Q: Does not the almanac say that the moon had disappeared by eleven o'clock?

A: (No answer.)

The defendant was acquitted. The almanac was probably for the correct year (a copy of it is available at the Harvard library), but Lincoln's characterization of its *contents* was somewhat misleading: the almanac does describe that night's moon as barely past the first quarter, and the implication of that description is that its lighted portion was barely more than one fourth. But a more careful review of the almanac disclosed that the lighted portion exceeded three fourths of the moon; it was nearly fully lighted. And it did not disappear until several hours after the witness had sworn he had seen the crime. (A check with the Harvard Observatory confirmed this.) But the witness was confused by Lincoln's misleading show of erudition and could not answer the questions. Lincoln apparently never informed the court of his misleading statements (if he was indeed aware, as I suspect he was, that they were misleading).